The Bible Answers Questions Children Ask

Linda R. McGinn

with T. R. Hollingsworth

THE BIBLE ANSWERS QUESTIONS *CHILDREN* ASK

A RESOURCE FOR *CARING* ADULTS

BROADMAN PRESS
NASHVILLE, TENNESSEE

© Copyright 1992 ● Broadman Press

All Rights Reserved

4250-92

ISBN: 0-8054-5092-0

Dewey Decimal Classification: 248.82

Subject Heading: CHILDREN - RELIGIOUS LIFE

Library of Congress Catalog Card Number: 91-21863

Printed in the United States of America

Library of Congress Cataloging-in-Publication Data

McGinn, Linda R., 1953-

    The Bible answers questions children ask / Linda R. McGinn.

      p.   cm.

    ISBN: 0-8054-5092-0

      1. Children–Religious life–Miscellanea. 2. God–Biblical

teaching–Miscellanea.   I. Title.

BV4571.2.M348 1992

268' .432–dc20

91-21863

CIP

To my precious children
Ruth, John, and Sarah
whose love and encouragement I cherish

"Delight yourself in the LORD and
he will give you the desires of
your heart" (Ps. 37:4).

and to my husband, Sam,
for seeking with me to exemplify God's love

Contents

Acknowledgments

Words are not adequate to express my appreciation to T. R. Hollingsworth for her depth of insight reflected in her writing of the *Implications for Older Children* sections and for her tireless assistance in editing and completing the final manuscript.

Introduction

"Mom, will you be with me in heaven?" three-year-old Sarah blurted out one morning.

Quite surprised, I paused for a moment and replied carefully.

"Well, Sarah, I plan to be there. God promises that if we believe in Jesus Christ, His Son, we will be with Him in heaven one day."

"I *know that* Mom," Sarah said with a hint of irritation at my lack of understanding. "I just mean when I get there will you be there?"

"I think I will be there before you get there, Sarah," I answered, wondering about my daughter's real concern.

"Good. I was afraid I'd get lost in the crowd. You'll hold my hand won't you?" Sarah grinned cheerfully at my nod of assurance and returned to her bowl of cereal.

Children's questions and concerns are often unpredictable. Sometimes it is perplexing to communicate answers in concrete terms that a child can understand. At the same time, we, as adults, are often amazed at children's depth of thought. We want to give accurate answers that are sensitive and comforting while anticipating deeper needs and possible unspoken anxieties.

As a mother of three and a pastor's wife for fourteen years, I am often approached by parents who are seeking biblical answers to their children's questions. I see the need for a resource tool for parents, grandparents, day-care workers, Sunday School teachers, or anyone who spends time with children. To meet this need, I've used Scripture verses and scriptural principles to formulate practical, easily understood answers for the children in our lives.

The Bible Answers Questions Children Ask is comprised of six main sections: questions about feelings, family and friends, actions, attitudes, faith, and the Person of God Himself. Each question is stated, an approximate adult response offered, and additional Scripture verses relating to the question supplied for more in-depth discussion with the child. At times, further insights from well-known authors are included. Following this, the heading *Implications for the Older Child* provides answers regarding the specific needs of pre-teen and adolescent children with related Scripture verses and again insightful information on each subject drawn from the writings of respected professionals.

In *The Bible Answers Questions Children Ask,* you will find answers in the Bible to satisfy your child's curiosity, offer reassurance when needed, and stimulate him to increase his understanding of God. God alone has answers for every question. Join me in seeking His wisdom as we endeavor to apply His Word to the specific needs found in our children's hearts.

Section I
Does God Care About Me?
Questions About Feelings

Section I
Does God Care About Me?
Questions About Feelings

A child's perception of the world is largely shaped by feelings. These feelings are in direct response to individuals and situations that touch his life.

This is simply illustrated by the child who is reluctant to return to an unfamiliar nursery where he or she has been harshly reprimanded. Such feelings of fear may carry over to similar situations in other settings.

On the other hand, the warmth of a grandparent's hug and kiss makes their home a safe place for the child. He or she anticipates a return visit with pleasure. Ross Campbell writes in *How to Really Love Your Child,*

> Remember that a child is much more emotional than cognitive, He therefore remembers feelings much more readily than facts. A child can remember how he felt in a particular situation much easier than he can remember the details of what went on.[1]

Since God cannot be met through the human senses, often a child does not have the experiences or the feelings that help form views of God. God may seem elusive and out-of-touch with every-day activity. In the book *Heavenly Humor for All God's Children,* one California teacher tells about the time she asked a student, "What do you think God looks like?"

"An 'unexplantable' figure" was the child's quick response.[2]

Caring adults can help change misconceptions about God. By touching a child's feelings with human love and caring and then relating these feelings to God Himself, soon God becomes a real Person to the child, one with feelings, interests, and compassionate concern. The child will learn that God knows him and, more importantly, loves him. Anne Gillilard writes:

> What *do* preschoolers learn from adults? Feelings and attitudes. These are caught by the young child—one does not have to say a word! In fact, one of the best ways we teach is through unspoken communication . . . . It is the touch of the hand, the friendly glance, the smile and the warmth of personality that speaks forcefully to the child.[3]

This knowledge of God's personal love experienced through an adult's example gives a positive sense of worth, crucial to the healthy development of every child. Richard Strauss in *Confident Children and How They Grow* writes:

> It is our inescapable conclusion, both from the Word of God and from human experience, that a child has the divinely bestowed right to feel secure in his parents' love. It is God's way of getting him started on the road to healthy emotional growth. It is God's security blanket for children.[4]

Every child may not have this opportunity for parental love, and you may be the adult God has chosen to touch a child's life with His love. I hope the answers provided to the following questions about feelings will aid you in giving confident reassurance of God's love to that special child in your life.

1

How Do I Know God Loves *Me?*

Ellen smiled as her daughter Susan snuggled close in her daddy's arm. Settled deep in the old worn easy chair, the two were almost hidden by the huge open book of Bible stories.

Ellen's thoughts drifted. Times had not been easy lately. Since Bob started his new job, simply paying the bills had been difficult. She had learned to stretch the vegetable soup over several days and to mend frayed hand-me-downs for Susan.

The economic recession weighed heavily on her as well as Bob, but Ellen was confident that their love for God and each other would see them through.

Bob was shocked and pleased when his boss called him in and offered him a substantial raise soon after the move. Ellen knew now that leaving their home and moving to Florida had been a wise decision after all. She silently thanked God for His care and provision.

Bob's words broke into Ellen's reminiscing. "Yes, Susan, God is faithful and answers our prayers when we wait on Him. He cares for and loves all His children." His deep voice was warm and loving as he closed the book. Lifting Susan into his arms, Bob headed for the bedroom to tuck her in for the night.

As the sound of Bob's footsteps faded, Ellen continued to reflect on her last weeks. Susan's adjustment to the move had been slow. She was a shy child, and other children seemed reluctant to make friends. Her Northern accent didn't help matters either.

Susan was gradually adjusting. She'd become more cheerful lately after two little girls began to seek her out.

Ellen was thankful for that but noticed Susan still clung to her sometimes and needed extra attention.

She needs reassuring right now, Ellen mused. *In this time of transition, my little kindergartner needs to feel loved, to know that God loves her.*

She thought of the Bible story Bob had just read aloud. He had chosen wisely. It spoke of God's never-changing love for His children.

"A penny for your thoughts." Bob said with a broad smile, as he reappeared in the doorway.

"I was just thinking . . ." she began.

Just then they heard feet pattering down the hallway. Susan's brown curls bobbed as she ran.

"I thought I just tucked you in bed, Young Lady," Bob said as he picked her up and hugged her close in his arms.

"Daddy," Susan responded, her brown eyes searching Bob's face. "Daddy, how do I know God loves *me?*"

Adult Response

The Bible says "God is love" (1 John 4:16). You know how much your mother and I love you. Did you know that God loves you even more than we ever could? That's because God *is* love. His love is much greater than we could ever share with you.

God's love even has a special name—*agape. Agape* love is a forever love that is God's alone. It's a love that never changes. No matter what you do or say, what you think or feel, God will always love you. God told the prophet Jeremiah, "I have loved you with an everlasting love; I have drawn you with loving-kindness" (Jer. 31:3). "Everlasting" means "forever" and God wants you to know He loves you as you are. He loves you because He made you.

Did you know God made you? He's the one who gave you your bright eyes and curly, long hair. He made you exactly the way you are and He loves you.

Additional Verses

1. "He is my loving God" (Ps. 144:2).
2. "Yet my unfailing love for you will not be shaken . . . says the Lord who has compassion on you" (Isa. 54:10).
3. "We know how much God loves us because we have felt his love and because we believe him when he tells us that he loves us dearly" (1 John 4:16, TLB).
4. "But from everlasting to everlasting the Lord's love is with those who fear him " (Ps. 103:7).

Further Insights

In their book *Parents & Children*, Ray and Anne Ortland write,

> . . . your children need unconditional love, the same kind of love God has for you. They need to hear you say, "We have loved you; we do love you, we will always love you"—and to know without a doubt nothing will ever change that commitment of love.
>
> That's how your Heavenly Parent treats you! He looks at you through Christ-colored glasses! He says, I have provided My Son for your righteousness, and I see you as perfect in Him. Then you have the courage to grow up to what He says you already are![5]

Paul Heiderbrecht, in his article, "Building Self-Esteem in Your Child," says,

> They (parents) must show their children that God is a loving Father—their own example is the best way to show this. For children to have good feelings about themselves, they must be able to relate to God's kindness and mercy. If they see God as distant or tyrannical, it becomes more difficult for them to appreciate themselves.[6]

Implications for the Older Child

As youngsters reach adolescence, emotions become more confused; self-image is challenged; and the need for love and acceptance is heightened. The realization and significance of God's unconditional and unfailing love becomes an imperative.

God's unconditional love exemplified in the love of parents and/or trusted adults acts as an anchor for the teenager amidst unsettling experiences and emotions. He needs to know that if all else fails, God's love remains sure.

One of the most supportive aspects of God's love is that it is not blind. God's love is not contingent upon or limited to behavior. God demonstrated His greatest act of love by sending His Son Jesus Christ to all of us, "while we were still sinners" (Rom. 5:8). At a time when teenagers are so acutely aware of inadequacies, inconsistencies, and other character flaws, it is a great comfort for them to realize that God was not oblivious to sin when He sent Jesus to Earth.

God's immeasurable love brought the solution to sin, providing forgiveness through belief in His Son's death and resurrection as well as the promise of new life in Him.

2
Sometimes I Feel Sad Inside. Does God Care?

Adult Response

God gave you feelings so that you can experience everything life holds for you. He wants you to be able to feel the joy in life. This also means that sometimes you'll feel sad.

Did you know that God understands your feelings because He has had those same feelings, too? The Bible tells us in John 11:35 that "Jesus wept."

God not only understands your sad feelings but He

wants to help you. Paul, an apostle (follower) of Jesus Christ called God, "the God of all comfort" in 2 Corinthians 1:3. *The New International Version* reads, "Praise be to the God, . . . who comforts us in all our troubles, so that we can comfort those in any trouble with the comfort we ourselves have received from God."

Do you want to receive comfort from God right now? Feeling sad is a normal emotion. Why don't you pray and talk to God? Ask Him for His comfort. Would you like me to pray with you now or would you rather be alone?

Don't forget God loves you. He understands your sad feelings and He wants to help you. I love you, too. If you decide you want to talk some more and tell me what is bothering you, I'm ready to listen.

Additional Verses

1. "Cast your cares on the Lord and he will sustain you; he will never let the righteous fall" (Ps. 55:22).

2. "Here on earth you will have many trials and sorrows; but cheer up, for I have overcome the world" (Jesus' words in John 16:33, TLB).

3. "You have seen me tossing and turning through the night. You have collected all my tears and preserved them in your bottle! You have recorded every one in your book" (Ps. 56:8, TLB)

4. "The Lord is good. When trouble comes, he is the place to go! And he knows everyone who trusts in him!" (Nah., 1:7, TLB)

Further Insights

In *Discipline Them, Love Them,* Betty N. Chase writes:

> When your child comes to you and wants to talk for a short period of time, if you genuinely look at your child and focus on him, he feels loved, special, encouraged and satisfied. However, if you are distant and remote from

your child when he comes to you, the child feels frustrated, disappointed, ignored, and perhaps in the way.[7]

Pat Hershey Owen says:

In order to really communicate when you converse with your child, you must first listen to the words he says; second, determine exactly what was behind his verbalization; and third, continue the conversation in such a way that you are able to prove to him that you understand,[8]

Ross Campbell, in *How to Really Love Your Child*, writes:

What is focused attention? Focused attention is *giving a child our full, undivided attention in such a way that he feels without doubt that he is completely loved.* That he is valuable enough in his own right to warrant parents' undistracted watchfulness, appreciation, and uncompromising regard. In short, focused attention makes a child feel he is the most important person in the world in his parents' eyes.[9]

Implications for the Older Child

During adolescence, confusing emotions begin to surface, and a child needs the assurance of your love and availability. You exemplify God's ever-present love when you offer this to your child. If you sense a teenager is in need of advice or concern, take time out immediately to listen and discuss these concerns. In this way, you communicate to him/her that his/her needs are important to you. No matter how trivial these concerns may seem, do not treat them as insignificant.

Sometimes an older child may not always be ready to confide in a parent or in another adult. He needs time alone to think. If after giving him this time, he still seems troubled, approach him gently at an opportune time. Assure him of your confidentiality. It is best to talk with him privately in his room away from other siblings or family members. Let him know that you are a trusted confidant and friend. Your godly support will offer tremendous comfort in difficult times.

3
How Do I Know God Is Really with Me?

Holly raced to the kitchen and grabbed the receiver. After replacing it, she hung her head and stumbled toward her bedroom, trying to hide her tears of disappointment. Carol had canceled.

Her mother followed her into the room. "Holly, is everything OK? What happened?"

Holly buried her head in the pillow.

"Holly, precious, what's wrong? Is Carol all right?"

Tears streamed down Holly's face. "Carol can't come. Her family decided to go out of town for the day to visit an aunt and Carol's mom says she has to go," she whispered. "Mom, I'm so lonely. John and Carrie play with their friends all the time and I never get to. I'm always alone."

Tenderly her mother wiped away the tears. "Honey, I'm sorry you feel lonely. It's hard when your brother and sister have more friends who live nearby. You know Dad and I love you dearly, but I know sometimes that's not enough. There is one Person who is always with you and who loves and cares for you even more than Dad and I ever could. You know who I'm speaking of, don't you?" she questioned softly.

"I know you mean God. But how do I know God is really with me? Can He take away my lonely feelings?"

Adult Response

Even though we feel alone at times, God tells us in the Bible that He is always with us. In Psalm 139:7-10 David says to God,

> Where can I go from your Spirit? Where can I flee from your presence? If I go up to the heavens, you are there.... If I rise on the wings of the dawn, if I settle on the far side of the sea, even there your hand will guide me, your right hand will hold me fast.

God never leaves us. The Bible also says that God watches over us, that He never sleeps. He is concerned about the things that happen in our lives and takes care of us night and day. "Indeed, he who watches over Israel will neither slumber nor sleep" (Ps. 121:4).

God is not only with you, He cares about you. He wants you to know He is always with you no matter where you are or what you are doing. He cares about things that concern you, and He wants you to talk with Him about your hurts and disappointments as well as joys and successes. Zephaniah 3:17 reads, "The Lord your God is with you.... He will take great delight in you, he will quiet you with his love, he will rejoice over you with singing."

God wants to be your best friend. Can you imagine that? He is not only always with you and caring about you, He wants to become your best friend. When you believe in Jesus, God's Son, Jesus becomes a friend who will never let you down. Jesus says in John 15:14, "You are my friends if you do what I command." He's there when you need Him and always listens to your thoughts and concerns when you pray and talk with Him. So you are never alone.

Jesus is right here with you now. He knows how disappointed and lonely you feel. Why don't you talk with Him about it? Ask Him to take away the loneliness. Ask Him to help you understand. You know that best friends talk about the things that really matter to them. It's the same in becoming Jesus' best friend. Talk to Him and tell Him how you feel. Ask Him to help you know how to be a better friend to Him by including Him in every part of your life. He wants you to.

Additional Verses

1. "And be sure of this—that I am with you always, even to the end of the world" (Matt. 28:20, TLB).

2. "For the Lord loves justice and fairness, he will never abandon his people" (Ps. 37:28, TLB).

3. "Because God has said, 'Never will I leave you,' never will I forsake you" (Heb. 13:5).

Further Insights

W. Herbert Scott writes,

> There is great comfort for the lonely in knowing that we have in heaven a divine friend and interceding high priest who knows all about loneliness and forsakenness (Hebrews 4:15-16). Prayer is God's way for us to avail ourselves of the companionship and sympathy of our heavenly Savior and praying Friend.[10]

Implications for the Older Child

Loneliness can be a particularly serious problem for the adolescent. It is more often a type of isolation. The adolescent struggles with the emotions and feelings of childhood: dependency versus responsibility. He searches to know himself and find out "who he is" in relation to the world around him.

This constant internal self-examination can cause him to become confused and withdrawn. He is a "spectator" in the world in which he lives. These emotions intensify as the attitudes and responses of his peers either affirm or undermine his sense of self-worth and purpose.

The greatest gift you can give a child at this time is the

assurance of support and the desire to listen. Remind the young person that God loves him and understands his deepest innermost needs. Even the older child needs to realize God is ever-present and has an intimate concern for the affairs of his life.

Tips for the Adult Dealing with an Adolescent

1) Assure the child of your availability. Keep lines of communication open. Without appearing to "pry," take time to sit and talk with your child. Ask gently about the things you think concern him.

2) Monitor your response to your child's thoughts. Don't appear "shocked" at his ideas which could preclude further discussion. Show that you respect the child's right to an opinion.

If you disagree with his observations or opinions, discuss your conclusions calmly and without appearing judgmental or critical. Pray that God will give him insight, understanding, and guidance. Trust in your child's ability to face issues, admit errors, and change views.

3) Never try to force your child to conform to your views. You have a right to expect him/her to comply with the standards you set in your home as long as he lives under your roof, but you cannot demand that he accept all of your thoughts and ideas without critical evaluation. To expect this is almost guaranteed to alienate your teenage child. He needs the freedom to arrive at his own conclusions. Your job is to be an example of God's love, concern, and trust.

4) Affirm your trust in the child regularly. Offer him opportunities to make definite decisions where the possible consequences are less threatening. You are then helping him to act wisely when more significant decision-making arises.

5) Listen, listen, and listen again with love, affirmation, and prayer. This is your greatest weapon against adolescent loneliness and isolation!

In *Focus on Family Life,* Gladys M. Hunt writes,

> Everyone knows loneliness. The most gregarious person you know has times of intense aloneness when there seems to be no one who understands, no one who can reach inside to the real person . . . . And that restless, lonely feeling is part of God's design. The empty spot within is a God-shaped hole, and only He can really fill it. Man's aloneness is relieved only when God becomes the center of his life.[11]

4
Sometimes I Am Afraid. Is God with Me Then?

Adult Response

Fears are very normal. We all feel fear at times. God gave us a type of "protective fear" so we will avoid things that might hurt us. Being afraid of uncontrolled fire is an example of God's "protective" fear.

But God does not want us to be afraid of the unknown. God says in the Bible, "So do not fear, for I am with you; do not be dismayed, for I am your God. I will strengthen you and help you; I will uphold you with my righteous right hand" (Isa. 41:10). God is always with you. He says He will never leave you and we know God always tells the truth. No matter what causes you to be afraid, God is right there taking care of you and watching over you. He wants you to trust Him, not to be afraid.

The Bible clearly tells us "The Lord himself goes before

you and will be with you; he will never leave you nor forsake you. Do not be afraid, do not be discouraged" (Deut. 31:8).

Let's talk about your fears and tell God about them, too. We know He'll hear our prayers.

Additional Verses

1. "The Lord is my light and my salvation—whom shall I fear? The Lord is the stronghold of my life—of whom shall I be afraid?" (Ps. 27:1).

2. "In my distress I prayed to the Lord and he answered me and rescued me. He is for me! How can I be afraid? What can mere man do to me? The Lord is on my side, he will help me" (Ps. 118:5-7, TLB).

3. "There is no fear in love. But perfect love drives out fear" (1 John 4:18).

Further Insights

Eileen Guder says in *Deliver Us from Fear,*

> We must look our fears in the face. Some of them will turn out to be exactly like a big black dog; menacing in appearance, but on closer examination we will find that the danger was in our own minds. There are other fears far more real. When Christ said, "Fear not," he meant those fears as well as the imaginary ones. Once we face them, we will find there is a way to be rid of them, and then we will be really free![12]

Implications for the Older Child

The fears of adolescents are rarely practical. They usually relate to the opinions of family and friends and have a narrow, self-conscious focus. Adults often see these fears as trivial, but they are very real to the child.

Some typical adolescent fears might be:

• What if my outfit is so different from my friend's that I'll stand out?

- What if I can't think of anything to say to my date?
- What if *nobody* asks me to the party?

Helping teenagers with initial fears of peer rejection could further offset more serious problems.

Problems which most adults see as significant, such as the effects of alcohol and drug abuse, are ignored by teenagers with words such as "that will never happen to *me*." Yet, when the initial fears of peer pressure go unchecked, it is then that a teenager seeks acceptance through involvement in such detrimental activities.

Parents need to remember that real fear lurks behind seemingly superficial concerns. An important way we can help our child deal with these is by preparing him for situations he might face.

When I was a teenager, my mother helped me by taking time to create hypothetical situations I might face and talking about possible ways to handle each one. Primarily, she simply described her personal adolescent experiences and explained how she handled them. Many she described were new to me. It was surprising how many of these exact situations I later faced, and I remember my gratitude to her and God for the wisdom to take the necessary action.

For example, one fear I had as a teenager was wondering what I would do if I were offered an alcoholic drink. I didn't want to drink but at the same time I desperately did not want to be ridiculed and ostracized by my peers. She said her solution was to respond quite adamantly when offered an alcoholic beverage, "Frankly, I can't stand the taste of it! I can't imagine why anyone would drink that when they could have a soft drink." It still amazes me that every person to whom I gave that response accepted it and dropped the subject. Many knew I held other convictions that kept me from drinking but that answer made the issue a matter of personal choice rather than one of intimidation over values. Often others would follow my lead, finding that they, too, could take a stand.

Remember to tell your teenager that in all circumstances Jesus Christ is right with him and He will "show you how to escape temptation's power" (1 Cor. 10:13, TLB) as well as help you through the situation. The deeper fears of life which teenagers face such as "Who am I?" or "What will I do in life?" can only be dealt with by leading your child into a deeper relationship with God and trust in His care.

God says in Jeremiah 29:11 " 'For I know the plans I have for you, declares the Lord, plans to prosper you and not to harm you, plans to give you hope and a future.' " Encourage your child to become active in church-related activities, to select Christian friends in school and church. Help him to become an example to his peers rather than an easy follower negatively influenced by others' seeming strength.

Further Insights

Elizabeth Skoglund writes about an openness necessary when discussing teenage fears in *Can I Talk to You?*

Openness in stating our beliefs and feelings is important in helping teenagers. When we talk with them, we should make it plain that we intend to be honest, and that we expect the same from them. This means admitting when we are wrong and letting them say what they wish to say—without becoming angry or rejecting.[13]

Tony Campolo says in "How Peer Pressure Works,"

Peer pressure is an easily misunderstood term. We think that a peer group tries to pressure an individual to conform. The truth is quite the opposite. The group does not pressure. The child, trying to gain acceptance, works very hard to find out what the group expects and deliberately wills to be like the group. The child hopes the group will then love and accept him. Conformity is not forced on the child; he actively seeks it. In reality, most groups are very tolerant of nonconformity—most groups enjoy deviants. But the child says, 'I want to do what they do and look the way they look so they will accept me.'"[14]

5

Sometimes I Make So Many Mistakes at School I Feel Worthless—Like a Total Failure. Does God Think I'm Worthless, Too?

Tim sat, body tense and erect, head down, and stared at his desk. *Please, please don't call on me today,* he thought. He listened as Mrs. Murphy, his fourth-grade teacher called the children's names and asked each one to spell an assigned word. *Friday—I hate Friday. It always happens on Friday.*

Each week, the class had a spelling contest. Each week, no matter how hard he tried, Tim misspelled his word. His classmates snickered, expecting his struggle and failure.

Why can't I spell? What is wrong with my brain that it can't remember words. As hard as I try, I can't seem to remember the words on Friday.

His stomach tightened as Mrs. Murphy moved up and down the rows, calling words. She reached the first girl in his row.

"Amy, please spell *equator.*"

"E-Q-U-A-T-O-R," Amy carefully pronounced.

"Ben, *rescue,*" Mrs. Murphy said.

"R-E-S-C-U-E," Ben announced proudly. He grinned at Tim.

One more person and Tim's body tensed. There was no

escape. He stared at the pencil's angular yellow shape as he twirled it between his thumb and finger.

"Mary, spell expensive."

Mary hesitated. "E-X-P-E-N-S-I-V-E, " she spelled.

"Well done, Mary. Now, Tim, will you please spell *important?*" Tim looked up, swallowed, and cleared his voice. "I-N, no, I-M . . . P-O-R-T-E-N-T."

The expression on Mrs. Murphy's face answered his unspoken question. There was a murmur of laughter from the class. Wrong. His answer was wrong again.

"I'm sorry, Tim. Angela, will you please spell *important* for the class."

To Tim the remaining minutes of the class were blurred. Finally, the bell rang and school was dismissed.

Tim walked home slowly, his eyes down. He groped in his pocket for his key and let himself in the back door. Clicking on the TV, he lost himself in Superman cartoons.

Finally, his mom and dad returned from work. Dinner was quiet, with only a few bits of conversation.

Later, as he and his mother knelt by his bed for his nightly prayers, Tim decided to tell her about his problem.

"Mom, did you ever have trouble with spelling?" he said struggling for words. "Every Friday, when we have the spelling test, I miss the word. The other kids giggle and tease me. I really try, Mom, but I feel like a failure. I feel worthless.

"Does God think I'm worthless?"

Adult Response

How could you be worthless to God? He created you. You are precious to Him. You are so special that He loves you as if you were the only person on earth.

God's love is so great that He knows and loves you completely while loving everyone else as well. David writes in

Psalm 36:5, "Your love, O Lord, reaches to the heavens, your faithfulness to the skies." God's love has no limits.

God created each of us to be different. We each have things we are really good at doing and then there are things we don't do well. No one can be good at everything. Each of us is special in God's eyes. We are each unique. To show God we are thankful and love Him, we can use our special talents to please Him and to help others.

You may have difficulty spelling, but don't forget how clever you are at making things with your hands. Look at the tremendous buildings, airports, and other things you build with your construction blocks. You have an exceptional ability to design things. Maybe God plans for you to be an architect someday and use that gift to help others. Only God knows what your future will be. (Use an example applicable to your child.)

God knows and understands everything. He understands your problem with spelling and if you really practice your spelling words and learn them well, He will know you have done your best, even if you miss a word. So today, let's pray and ask Him to help you with your spelling.

Additional Verses

The Bible, in 1 John 4:9, tells us "God showed how much he loved us by sending his only Son into this wicked world to bring to us eternal life through his death." That's total love.

1. "For you created my inmost being; you knit me together in my mother's womb. I praise you because I am fearfully and wonderfully made" (Ps. 139:13-14).

2. "Are not two sparrows sold for a penny? Yet, not one of them will fall to the ground apart from the will of your Father. And even the very hairs of your head are all numbered. So do not be afraid; you are worth more than many sparrows" (Matt. 10:29-31).

3. "Before I formed you in the womb I knew you, before you were born I set you apart" (Jer. 1:5).

4. "Look at the birds of the air; they do not sow or reap or store away in barns, and yet your heavenly Father feeds them. Are you not much more valuable than they?" (Matt. 6:26).

Further Insights

In *Hide or Seek*, James Dobson says there are ways to teach a child of his genuine significance, that every child is entitled to hold up his head, not in haughtiness and pride, but in confidence and security. "This is the concept of human worth intended by our Creator. How foolish for us to doubt our value when He formed us in His own image!"[15]

He suggests that parents work with their children as allies on their behalf. When a child is upset, a parent can intervene and give him the necessary implements needed to help him succeed. "One of these vital tools," he says, "involves a process called compensation. It means the individual counterbalances his weaknesses by capitalizing on his strengths."[16]

By doing this, a parent can help the child discover the areas where he will excel, supporting him as he tackles new challenges.

Implications for the Older Child

Identity quest is one of the principal adolescent issues. Each child has a deep need to feel loved, valued, and unique in the eyes of the family, respected adults, and friends. Yet, the struggle for independence is also a motivating factor. Maturity grows out of this "pulling away," but it can cause separation between the teen and those whose approval he needs and wants.

The teenager's search for identity causes a deep desire

for popularity and approval. Peers are not a source of support and encouragement. Many times their critical and demeaning opinions can cause irreparable harm. To meet the criticism, it's essential that a teen have some areas where he excels. Dobson says,

> There is nothing more risky than sending a teenager into the storms of adolescence with no skills, no unique knowledge, no means of compensating. When this occurs, his ego is stark naked. He cannot say, I may not be the most popular student in school, but I am the best trumpet player in the band! His only source of self esteem comes from acceptance of other students—and their love is notoriously fickle.[17]

In "Every Kid Needs an Adult Friend," Wayne Rice instructs us to,

> Support programs in your church or community that allow teenagers the opportunity to be around adults who understand them and are willing to enter into positive relationships with them. Adults who care about teenagers aren't easy to find. But every teenager needs a friend like that.[18]

When failures occur, the parent can guide the teen to understand that God knows he will not always be successful. Giving his best is what pleases God. Failures are simply new beginnings. We learn from failures and are motivated to pursue new and different areas of interest where potential may lie.

Consistent encouragement and reinforcement of their special worth in God's eyes is invaluable during these years. When a teen questions the value of life itself and his place in it, it is imperative that he has a firm sense of his purpose and worth to God. Ephesians 2:10 says, "For we are God's workmanship, created in Christ Jesus to do good works, which God prepared in advance for us to do."

The adolescent needs to know God loves him, created him, and knows him as an individual. God values him, and has a plan for his life. These truths are indispensable for the young person who is dealing with the insecurities of adolescence.

6
Does God Care That I'm Sick?

Adult Response

God cares about everything that happens to you. He is with you and wants to give you His comfort and encouragement. In Philippians 4:19 Paul writes, "And my God will meet all your needs according to his glorious riches in Christ Jesus."

God doesn't want you to feel bad, to have a fever, headache, and so forth, but these things do happen to us. We must learn to accept days when we aren't feeling as well or happy as we like. Always remember, "For he does not willingly bring affliction or grief to the children of men" (Lam. 3:33).

God gives doctors wisdom to understand your needs. He has provided knowledge about medicines that may hasten your recovery. Most of all, He gives you Himself—His very presence to strengthen you and help you when you are discouraged.

As we've learned, you are never alone when difficult things happen in your life. Not only is God with you, actively involved in helping you, but He promises that if you love Him and trust Him, He can take even the worst circumstances and change them to produce good things in your life. Romans 8:28 says, "And we know that all that happens to us is working for our good if we love God and are fitting into his plans" (TLB).

So tell God how you feel when you hurt. Take time to learn about Him by reading His Bible. You will learn how He helped others who were sick or hurting.

Additional Verses

1. "Lord, you alone can heal me, you alone can save me, and my praises are for you alone" (Jer. 17:14, TLB).

2. "For he has not despised or disdained the suffering of the afflicted one; he has not hidden his face from him but has listened to his cry for help" (Ps. 22:24).

3. "The Lord will sustain him on his sickbed and restore him from his bed of illness" (Ps. 41:3).

4. "God has said, 'Never will I leave you; never will I forsake you' " (Heb. 13:5).

Further Insights

Judith Shelley, in *Parents and Children*, says,

The school-age child may find additional spiritual struggles during times of serious illness. Children from six to twelve are developing an increasingly sharp sense of right and wrong. They know they do bad things, and they feel guilty about it. They also expect immediate punishment for their guilt. Sometimes they secretly assume that their illnesses are punishment for a real or imagined wrong. It can be helpful to explore what they think caused their problems.

Children need assurance that God is not punishing them through their illnesses.

While parents and other caring adults have a strong influence on the spiritual development of children, we can also have confidence that God cares for sick children even more than we do. The Holy Spirit sometimes breaks into a child's world and gives a spiritual understanding well beyond the expected norm. Children seldom blame God for an illness or get angry with Him because of it. They often end up comforting the adults who care for them.

That is what sick children need most to know—that God

loves them. We demonstrate God's love by our own consistent care as well as by teaching them the Bible and how to pray. The spiritual needs of sick children are the same as those of well children; they are just a little closer to the surface.[19]

Elizabeth Catherine Baker-Smith writes in "The Impact of Illness on the Family and the Ministry of the Christian Community,"

If it is the child who is ill, many things are happening within and being done to his/her body which don't make sense in the world as he/she had come to understand it. Without explanation, the child begins to feel isolated.

Discussing such situations is difficult for the adults who are significant to the child because of their own anxieties and fears and their involvement with the child.

But with both children and adults, even just having the issue "in the open" for discussion makes it less frightening. The child should be encouraged to express his/her feelings and share what is causing anxiety.[20]

Implications for the Older Child

Illness is not confined to young children and adults. Teens, too, deal with illness as a part of life. This was seen in the March 1987 *Teen* magazine when several teens questioned Ray Rosen about psoriasis, tension, ulcers, car accident injuries, and bladder control.

The older child and adolescent needs to be able to communicate fears and concerns about illness. The concern and encouragement of parents and caring adults are essential. Encourage relatives and friends to support the child with cards, visits, or other thoughtful expressions of love to prevent the possibility of isolating the child by the illness.

One teen who was ill and missed an extended period of school was overjoyed one day to receive from her classmates a basket of get-well cards tied up with a bunch of bright-colored ribbons. The reminder that friends had not forgotten her and were praying for her did much to lift her spirits and quicken recovery. Any expression of love shown during times of sickness or trauma is rarely forgotten.

Remind your teen of the compassion that Jesus felt toward people suffering from various illnesses. He even healed someone on the Sabbath knowing that the Jewish leaders would use it against Him (Mark 3:1-6). Pray for healing in accordance with God's will.

7

Can I Know God Will Always Take Care of Me and Know My Needs?

Adult Response

God not only knows your material needs for food, shelter, and clothing, He also understands the deepest innermost needs of your heart. In the Bible, Jesus tells us,

> Don't worry about *things*—food, drink, and clothes. For you already have life and a body—and they are far more important than what to eat and wear. Look at the birds! They don't worry about what to eat—they don't need to sow or reap or store up food—for your heavenly Father feeds them. And you are far more valuable to him than they are. Will your worries add a single moment to your life? And why worry about your clothes? Look at the field lilies! They don't worry about theirs. Yet, King Solomon in all his glory was not clothed as beautifully as they. And if God cares so wonderfully for flowers that are here today and gone tomorrow, won't he more surely care for you? But your heavenly father already knows perfectly well that you need them, and he will give them to you if you

give him first place in your life and live as he wants you to
(Matt. 6:25-30,32-33, TLB)

We all have needs that God is constantly aware of and
caring for. We need to feel safe and loved. God promises
us that when we trust in Him, He becomes our "safe
place." He is always with us and nothing that happens in
our lives can separate us from Him. Paul tells us in Romans 8:38:

God takes even the bad things in our lives and works
them for out good if we love Him and give Him first place.
(See Rom. 8:28.)

For I am convinced that neither death nor life, neither
angels nor demons, neither the present nor the future, nor
any powers, neither height nor depth, nor anything else in
all creation, will be able separate us from the love of God
that is in Christ Jesus our Lord.

God always loves us, too. His love never ends. David
writes in the Bible, "But I trust in your unfailing love; my
heart rejoices in your salvation. I will sing to the Lord, for
he has been good to me" (Ps. 13:5).

Sometimes the things we think we need are not really
needs. We see something a friend has and we want it, too.
It's hard for us to know the difference between a need and
want, but God, who knows our heart and understands our
situation perfectly, knows exactly what we need. We can
trust Him to guide us in our choices and provide for our
real needs.

We have one need that is greater than any other—the
need to belong to God. God sent His Son Jesus Christ to
earth promising that if we believe in Him, we become
God's child and this greatest need in life is met forever.
Jesus says in John 10:10, "I have come that they may
have life and have it to the full."

Additional Verses

1. "Remember, your Father knows exactly what you need even before you ask him!" (Matt. 6:8, TLB).
2. " 'For I know the plans I have for you," says the Lord. 'They are plans for good and not for evil, to give you a future and a hope' " (Jer. 29:11)
3. "And God is able to make all grace abound to you so that in all things at all times, having all that you need, you will abound in every good work" (2 Cor. 9:8).

Further Insights

Norm Wakefield, in *A Happier Family*, identifies the values children need for us to communicate. One of these is the need to trust. He writes,

> Trusting in the Lord for all our life needs is a value of importance to us. It is a dimension of our family life-style which we deeply cherish for our children. Holding to this value brings security and peace to mind and heart. Depending for one's sufficiency in himself, in others or in material resources demonstrates a life value which will ultimately be disappointing.
>
> Perhaps more than any other value, our children need to see that trusting the Lord is an integral part of their parents' lives. The parents' deep and abiding confidence in the heavenly Father in the midst of difficult or seemingly impossible circumstances can make a lasting impression on the youngster.[21]

Ross Campbell, in *How to Really Love Your Child,* explains how we can show our children God's faithfulness to meet needs through examples in our daily life.

> A child needs to learn how God meets all personal and family needs, including financial. He needs to know what his parents are praying for. For example, he needs to know when you are praying for the needs of others. He should (again, as appropriate) know of problems for which you are asking God's help. And don't forget to keep him

informed about how God is working in your life, how He is using you to minister to someone. And, of course, a child should certainly know you are praying for him and for his individual, particular needs.[22]

Implications for the Older Child

A child's needs and his perception of those needs change as he matures. He begins to recognize deeper, sometimes confusing, needs within, often too complex to verbalize. Campbell says,

> This yearning is expressed by older children in many ways. One adolescent says he needs a meaning in life. Another wants a standard to guide her. Other seeking youngsters long for higher guidance, something to hold on to, or something to show them how to live.[23]

The need for a sense of purpose, direction, personal fulfillment, and meaning can only be found in a relationship with Jesus Christ Himself. He alone gives life meaning. Leading the adolescent to a relationship with God through Christ and encouraging him to find God's purpose for his life is the greatest gift you can give him/her at this time.

Jeremiah 29:11: " 'For I know the plans I have for you," says the Lord. 'They are plans for good and not for evil, to give you a future and a hope,' " is a reassuring statement for the teen.

Encourage young people to discover these plans by drawing closer to God. Remind them that though they may not understand all their feelings and needs, God understands and is working always to meet the deepest needs of their hearts.

Campbell says,

> As a child matures, we parents want to gradually increase sharing with him how we ourselves love God, walk daily with Him, rely on Him, seek His guidance and help,

thank Him for His love, care, gifts, and answered prayer.[24]

When his adolescent son suddenly burst out with the question, "Mom, what's wrong with me?" John Albright describes his wife's response.

Seizing the moment to move in close, my wife lovingly stroked his hair. He always liked that. She explained several things; that there was nothing wrong with him; that the uncertainty of his feelings was something he would be experiencing increasingly over the next few years; that he would gain skills to control those feelings; and that it was a natural part of growing up.[25]

Albright continues,

That is, perhaps, the greatest truth we parents can share with our children—the assurance that God created us, that God understands our ups and downs, and that God still loves and accepts us through it all. We know it because we are experiencing it; and our children will learn it from us as we model God's acceptance through our patience and understanding of them.[26]

8
Sometimes I Feel Ugly. How Can I Like Myself the Way God Made Me?

Golden autumn leaves crunched under Emily's feet as she skipped the short distance to the bus stop. She inhaled the smoky fragrance of burning firewood with delight. She watched curls of white smoke escape the chimneys of surrounding homes as the brisk morning air brushed against her face. Finally, the first day of school had arrived.

Emily smiled up at Mr. Hansen, the bus driver, as the

shiny yellow bus screeched to a halt and the doors flew open.

"Hello, Emily," he called with his friendliest grin. "Welcome to a new school year."

Climbing the stairs, Emily timidly searched for an empty seat and a familiar face. She spotted Kristen. Kristen and Emily had been friends last year—not as close friends as Emily had hoped, but friends anyway. They hadn't seen each other all summer.

Emily slipped into the seat beside Kristen, smoothing wrinkles from her crisp new plaid jumper.

"Hi, Kristen," she said with a smile.

"Hi, Emily. I almost didn't recognize you! Boy, do you look different. I never saw you with glasses before."

The smile faded from Emily's face. *Her glasses!*

Last spring as the school year ended, Mrs. Ellis, her teacher, had told Emily's mother about how Emily squinted at the blackboard. They visited the optometrist and Mrs. Ellis's suspicions were confirmed. Emily needed glasses.

On July third, Emily put on her new glasses for the first time. She'd never forget that day because the next day was the Fourth of July and the annual family picnic. Relatives gawked at her when they saw the glasses. Comments like: "Emily, I didn't know your eyes were bad;" "Maybe you won't have to wear those old glasses long;" "Emily, wearing glasses isn't that bad;" or "You'll get used to it" were repeated again and again. Then Sarah, Emily's least favorite cousin, made her unforgettable comment, "My, don't you look cute in glasses, Miss Four Eyes!" She said it with a mean grin.

Emily felt ugly. Uglier than she had ever felt before. She felt so ugly she looked away every time she glimpsed herself in a mirror.

July and August finally passed. Sometimes she even forgot Sarah's gibe when she was having fun or getting ready for school . . . until today. Emily stared down at her tightly clasped hands resting on her lap. Kristen stared at her as if she'd never seen her before. Emily said nothing. Sarah's taunting words at the picnic rang in her ears.

Arriving at school, Emily walked numbly through the remaining day. She rarely looked up hoping no one would notice her. The joy of renewed friendship, of colorful new books, of kind teachers, was dampened. Emily felt ugly. All she wanted to do was go home.

Rushing through the front door at home, Emily hid her tear-streaked face in the folds of her grandmother's skirt. She sobbed.

"Emily, what is it?" her grandmother asked gently. "What's wrong?"

"Nana, I feel so ugly!" she spoke between sobs. "I know you say God loves me the way I am. But how can I love myself when I feel so ugly?"

Adult Response

With God, there are no accidents or mistakes. What you might think is ugly, God sees as beautiful because He created you, loves you, and has special purposes for your life.

Author and speaker Elisabeth Elliot once told the story of a missionary woman, Gladys Ailworth. It seems that Gladys had two great sorrows as a child which she explained this way. "One was that all my friends had beautiful golden curls, my hair was black. And when all my friends were still growing, I stopped!" Being short and having dark hair was a great disappointment to Gladys.

Then, one day Gladys believed God wanted her to become a missionary to China. She prayed, prepared, and took a train across Europe and Russia headed for China.

Gladys finally arrived in Shanghai, China. Gladys said "I stood on the wharf looking around on all the people to whom Jehovah God had sent me. Every single one of them had black hair and every single one of them had stopped growing. And I said, 'Lord God, you know what you're doing!' "

God loves you as you are. More importantly, God cares about what you think, say, and feel in your heart. As you grow to know and love Him more, the beauty of your heart and the person you've become will shine through your face. Everyone is beautiful when they have God's love in their hearts.

Additional Verses

1. But the Lord said to Samuel, "Men judge by outward appearance, but I look at a man's thoughts and intentions" (1 Sam. 16:7, TLB).

2. "For you created my inmost being; you knit me together in my mother's womb. I praise you because I am fearfully and wonderfully made; your works are wonderful, I know that full well" (Ps. 139:13-14).

3. "Do not be concerned about the outward beauty that depends on jewelry, or beautiful clothes, or hair arrangement. Be beautiful inside, in your hearts, with the lasting charm of a gentle and quiet spirit which is precious to God" (1 Pet. 3:3-4, TLB).

4. "The Lord your God is with you, he is mighty to save. He will take great delight in you, he will quiet you with his love, he will rejoice over you with singing" (Zeph. 3:17).

Further Insights

James Dobson writes of the need to let your child know that God finds him lovable and special.

> If a child is odd or noticeably different, he has certainly heard about his deformity from his friends and neighbors during pre-school days. Without meaning to hurt others, children can be terribly brutal to one another. Some youngsters feel it their personal mission in life to point

out everyone else's flaws and deficiencies. Life can be very uncomfortable, indeed, for the child who is too fat or too thin, too tall or too short, or besieged by a tornado of freckles, . . . or whose hair is too curly or too straight, or one who has big feet or a crossed eye, or protruding ears, or any other noticeable distortion. The child's emotional reaction operates according to the weakest link in the chain; that is, he can be physically perfect except for a single embarrassing feature, and he will worry about that one deficiency as though it were the only important thing in life.[27]

In our story, the troubled child, Emily, turned to her grandmother. Sometimes a child may talk more freely to a grandparent whose love seems unconditional and unhurried. Grandparents have the potential to be a positive catalyst in the grandchildren's lives. Judson Swihart says,

> Grandparents can offer a special kind of love. Every child needs someone to love her unconditionally and maybe even irrationally. The people most likely to give that kind of love are grandparents.
>
> Grandparents transmit moral values. Most grandparents have a clear set of values; they know where they're coming from. Our culture has gone through an era of relativism, and in the general culture many parents are not sure what they believe. But grandparents usually have decided certain issues are either right or wrong, and they pass their values on to their grandchildren.[28]

Implications for the Older Child

Appearance is a primary focus of teenagers. Whether it is the clothes they wear, blemishes on their face, or their muscular physique, an all-encompassing thought is, "How do I look?" Teens struggle with self-acceptance. When they focus upon outward appearances, it is their way of asking, "Do you like me? Will you accept me?"

It is good to compliment the child at this age. Do not

harp on improving his/her appearance. Encouraging the use of heavy makeup or buying expensive clothes only confirms the young person's fears that he or she is indeed unsatisfactory.

A better approach to helping the adolescent is to identify and compliment character qualities which you admire and see developing in his/her life. Attitudes of integrity, honesty, and unselfishness, should be encouraged.

But to ignore his or her concern over appearance is to hide your head in the sands of ignorance. Remind your teen that you realize appearance is important to him/her. It may determine how she feels about herself and it may boost her self-confidence. Yet it is only a part of her as a person.

At times, being overly conscious of physical appearance may set the wrong priorities for her life, add additional worries and pressure at a time when the child is already stressed by body changes and feelings.

To help your teen present his most favorable appearance to his peers and teachers, encourage him to keep his skin clean and free of blemishes, if possible, by proper diet and skin care. Help him to maintain correct weight by cutting down on "junk" food and desserts. In a seventh-grade class, a shy boy arrived at school to find a bottle of mouthwash on his desk. Devastated by the thought of bad breath, he spoke with his hand over his mouth for days afterwards. Encourage your child to brush daily and see a dentist regularly. Bad breath is treatable.

Paul writes in Philippians 4:8 "Finally, brothers, whatever is true, whatever is noble, whatever is right, whatever is pure, whatever is lovely, whatever is admirable—if anything is excellent or praiseworthy—think about such things."

Anything you can do to help your child look past himself to the virtues of things with eternal significance and the needs of others will prove to be a great asset in the future. Our aim as parents should be to help our children become secure in their value as childred of God.

Section II
Is God Concerned About Relationships?
Questions About Family and Friends

Section II
Is God Concerned About Relationships?
Questions About Family and Friends

Each child begins a training program at birth which continues for a lifetime. It is often rigorous, confusing, hurtful, joyous, frustrating, and rewarding. It will have an impact on every aspect of his life as long as he lives. This training program is found in the "school of relationship building."

It starts at home. Family members comprise the first significant unit where relationships must be defined and developed. Miriam Huffman Rockness in *Keep These Things—Ponder Them in Your Heart* says:

> Through this intense daily contact (with family) not only do we find the opportunity to develop skills in relating to others, but something positive can happen to our own self as well. Elizabeth Elliot says, "and it is in relation to other people that we ourselves become full persons." Our selfish persons are shaped and refined as we come up against the wills and needs of other people in a situation we cannot easily walk out on.[1]

It is important that we be sensitive in this area as our children grow. Home should be a safe place where relationships are tested, mistakes can be forgiven, opportunities for trial and error experiences are possible.

Richard Strauss writes in *Confident Children and How They Grow*,

The homes where Jesus Christ reigns as Lord in the lives of every family member are the homes that will tower above the rest in love, serenity, happiness, mutual concern one for another, and the ability to adjust to people outside the home.[2]

When positive relationships are built within the family unit, the child is equipped to leave home and establish meaningful relationships with peers and those in authority outside the family.

God cares deeply about relationships. He sent His Son so the relationship with us, His creation, could be reestablished. He decreed that the spreading of the gospel of His Son be fulfilled through the relationships we have with others. We, through our united relationships, represent Christ to the world as His church, Christ's body.

Helping our children through the struggles and stresses of the "school of relationship building" will enable them to experience a fulfilling and meaningful life of purpose and accomplishment for Christ's kingdom on earth.

9

As a Christian, How Can I Make Friends Who Won't Make Fun of Me and Hurt Me? Who Are the Kinds of Friends God Wants Me to Have?

Anna's shiny blond curls danced in the sunlight as she skipped through the skating rink parking lot. Stopping at the entrance, she touched a soft petal of one of the bright red tulips clumped in barrels announcing spring's arrival. Rhythmic melodies escaped through the open door, welcoming her as she breathed in the fragrant April air.

Anna loved to skate but she found birthday skating parties really special. Today was her friend Sam's tenth birthday and she could hardly wait. Laughter greeted her as she entered. Her friends were giggling with excitement as the attendant fitted skates.

"Hi, Anna!" Sam waved and called as he turned to talk with the boy next to him. Anna paused, suddenly apprehensive as she looked at the crowd of strange faces.

"Hey, Kid," a boy called out, "Are you with Sam's party?" Anna reluctantly nodded "yes."

"Come over here and get your skates. You're holding us up. We can't start until everyone is ready." Anna hurried toward the stranger who glared as she approached. After trying several pairs, the attendant finally found one to fit.

When she thought he wasn't looking, Anna stared at the boy who'd called to her. Taller than Anna, he seemed to be about twelve or thirteen. His hair was uncombed, his face unwashed, and he frowned impatiently as he waited.

Could this be one of Sam's friends? she thought. Then she noticed that when they began to skate, the boy shoved

55

the others aside and, head down, pushed ahead of everyone.

Then it happened. Sam, a new skater, groped along the edge of the ring, hugging the rail to keep from falling. Suddenly one leg flew out from under him and he slipped to the floor. At that moment, the guy who had called to Anna sped by and tripped over Sam's extended foot.

Sliding across the floor, unharmed, the older boy shouted angrily, "How dare you trip me, you creep! Why don't you learn to skate? You tripped me on purpose."

Sam struggled to his feet and grasped the rail. Frightened, he cowered as the bully shouted, his fist raised. "Come on and fight, you nerd." At that moment, the manager angrily dragged the boy from the rink. Anna watched as they headed for the man's office.

With a weak smile, Anna said, "Sam, why did you pick him to be your friend?"

Sam winced with regret.

"That's OK," Anna responded. "You'll make a better choice next time."

Adult Response

I know it's hard at times to make friends. But the friends you choose are very important to God. Jesus wants to be your best friend. He tells you, "You are my friends if you do what I command. I have called you friends, for everything that I learned from my Father I have made known to you" (John 15:14-15).

Jesus is your Friend (if you belong to Him) and He wants you to make best friends with others who love Him, too. They will help you think and act in a way that pleases God. They will want to follow Jesus' example just like you.

There will be times when Christian friends will disappoint you or hurt your feelings. Try to remember that they aren't perfect and are sinners just like you. Forgive your friend. Love her/him and pray for him.

Don't be surprised if friends reject or hurt you. These children need your love, forgiveness, and kindness even when it's hard to give.

When Jesus lived on earth, people hurt Him, too. Jesus said, "If you belong to the world, it would love you as its own. As it is, you do not belong to the world, but I have chosen you out of the world. . . . If they persecuted me, they will persecute you also" (John 15:19-20).

"Friends are friends forever when the Lord is Lord of them," writes Michael W. Smith. Remember that Jesus is your "forever" friend, and He helps you become the kind of friend He desires you to be.

Additional Verses

1. "A friend loves at all times" (Prov. 17:17).
2. "Greater love has no one than this, that he lay down his life for his friends" (John 15:13).
3. "A man of many companions may come to ruin, but there is a friend who sticks closer than a brother" (Prov. 18:24).

Implications for the Older Child

Many parents move away from the older child, focusing their attention on the youngest members of the family. They assume the older child is capable of handling his affairs. Too, they want to give him or her opportunities to develop independence and maturity. They may assume that making lasting friends isn't of prime importance at this time in life.

Yet, most teachers and parents agree that the problem of friendship becomes a primary issue once the child leaves elementary school. Here peers have deciding influences on behavior. Torn between childhood and adulthood, the young boy or girl looks to peers for guidance.

Adults who work with this age agree that making friends is difficult for some teens. Many are cruel and unkind to one another. They form cliques and ignore or ostracize others. Thus many kids strive to copy the class leaders who may be the least likable members of the group. How can you help your child deal with rejection, unhappiness, and lack of acceptable friends?

Christian parents can help children make and keep friends during these difficult years by spending as much time as possible with them. A thoughtful adult is careful not to embarrass a child. Don't reprimand or criticize a son or daughter in front of friends, family, or strangers. Even praise must be appropriately given. One boy is quoted as saying, "I hate it when my parents say stuff in front of my friends, like how wonderful I am or what I've done."

So save your praise for times when you are alone. Remind your son or daughter that to have a friend, you must first be a friend. Jesus told His disciples, "Greater love has no one than this, that one lay down his life for his friends" (John 15:13). Paul wrote to the Philippians "Do not merely look out for your own personal interests, but also for the interests of others" (Phil. 2:4, NASB).

Encourage your older child to invite friends into your home. Control any urges you may have to interrogate the visitors about their personal life and views. Trust your teen to show Christian love and discernment.

Also, encourage your child to become active in the church youth program, to attend Sunday School and church services. A child who has opportunities to make friends within the church family is less likely to be overcome by the traumas of peer pressure. Remember that Jesus gave us a rule for treating friends. He said, "Do for others what you want them to do for you" (Matt. 7:12, TLB).

10

My Older Brother and Sister Tease Me and I Become So Angry I Feel Like Hitting Them. What Does God Think About Anger?

Mark slammed the door behind him as he angrily stalked out of the room. "You make me so mad!" he yelled. "You're always coming in and moving my things. Now I can't find my baseball. Sisters! Sometimes I wish girls had never been invented!"

He stomped across the dining room, brown eyes gleaming and lips tense. His dad's calm voice stopped him as he passed by the living room door.

"Come here, Son," he said. Mark entered the room, still red-faced with anger.

"Mark, your sister was wrong to move your things without asking, but you must get in control of your anger. You call yourself a Christian, Son. As one, you can't continue to behave like this."

"But, Dad!" Mark countered. "I know I'm a Christian. Christians still get mad sometimes, don't they? Carrie was wrong to hide my ball. Anyway, what *does* God think about anger?"

Adult Response

Everyone gets angry at times, and all anger is not wrong. Paul says, "In your anger, do not sin" (Eph 4:26). There is a "righteous" anger that is opposed to evil actions which reject God and His Word. Then there is an anger that helps us express our frustration without hurting ourselves and others.

Most anger does not fit these categories and is not pleasing to God. It is hurtful and destructive. Angry words cause pain and sometimes heartache that takes months and sometimes years to heal. The old rhyme "Sticks and stones may break my bones, but words can never hurt me" is a lie. Cruel words can hurt us inside more deeply than sticks or stones could ever hurt us on the outside. Our skin heals easily but wounds of the heart may take years to heal. In some cases only God's love and forgiveness can heal our inner hurts.

James tells us, "My dear brothers, take note of this: Everyone should be quick to listen, slow to speak and slow to become angry, for man's anger does not bring about the righteous life that God desires" (Jas. 1:19).

Every one of us gets angry sometimes, but God gives us a special power to control anger. It is the power of the Holy Spirit living in your heart. When we ask Jesus Christ to live in our hearts, He gives us His Holy Spirit. Do you know what gift the Holy Spirit offers to you? Paul tells us, "But the fruit of the Spirit is *love,* joy, peace, *patience,* kindness, goodness, faithfulness, gentleness and *self-control*"(Gal 5:22-23).

The Holy Spirit gives us the power to control our emotions. You can replace anger with love and patience. The next time your sister does something to make you angry, stop and pray, "Father, please help me to be calm, to listen and to handle this with the Holy Spirit's power in a way that pleases You." If you sincerely trust Him, the Holy Spirit will give you the love, patience, and self-control you need.

Additional Verses

1. "A fool gives full vent to his anger, but a wise man keeps himself under control. An angry man stirs up dissension, and a hot-tempered one commits many sins" (Prov. 29:11,22).

2. "Get rid of all bitterness, rage and anger, brawling and slander along with every form of malice. Be kind and

compassionate to one another, forgiving each other, just as in Christ God forgave you" (Eph. 4:31-32).

3. "Do not make friends with a hot-tempered man, do not associate with one easily angered, or you may learn his ways and get yourself ensnared" (Prov. 22:24-25).

4. "If anyone says, 'I love God,' yet hates his brother, he is a liar. For anyone who does not love his brother, whom he has seen, cannot love God whom he has not seen. And he has given us this command: Whoever loves God must also love his brother" (1 John 4:20-21).

Further Insights

In *Common Sense Discipline,* Roger Allen and Ron Rose say,

> Anger is a very natural emotion. When it is used to express the feelings of the moment, then it's a legitimate way to share our hurt and frustration. Anger is like a smoke detector that warns us we have a problem. The anger says loud and clear that something has caused hurt or frustration. When anger is used to attack, however, it becomes a weapon, and its design is to get someone to change his mind.[3]

Allen and Rose go on to say that children often use anger to gain control.

Ross Campbell, in *Kids Who Follow, Kids Who Don't,* writes, "We must, first of all, give our children unconditional love and prevent some of their anger, and then teach them to handle their natural anger."[4]

Implications for the Older Child

Anger is a normal human emotion, and sibling rivalry is a fact. When parents accept that, they are better able to deal with the anger of an older child. Remember that angry feelings do not vanish. Remind your child that everyone has periods of anger and that there are ways of expressing it without harming himself or another person.

Also reinforce the value that there is no place in your home for revenge and retaliation.

Often, an angry child will attempt to belittle the source of his anger by questioning his or her morals, intelligence, or abilities. By reminding your teenager of biblical references to anger, you may be able to help him see the destructive force of uncontrolled anger. "A gentle answer turns away wrath, but a harsh word stirs up anger" (Prov 15:1). Or Paul's advice to the Ephesians "In your anger do not sin; Do not let the sun go down while you are still angry, and do not give the devil a foothold" (Eph 4:26-27).

Encourage your teenager to express anger in nondestructive ways. When communication is open, talking about the reasons for anger can be helpful. By identifying the stress that caused the anger and searching for means of preventing it in the future, your child will be better able to recognize and deal with unexplainable and perhaps frightening emotions.

11

Why Should I Try to Be Kind to Someone When Everyone Else Rejects or Ridicules Him?

Adult Response

Everyone is special to God. He created us and loves us. His desire is that every person come to know His Son Jesus Christ. How will others come to know Jesus? By seeing God's love shining through your actions and attitudes.

If you remain silent while others are making fun of or rejecting someone, or if you join in, you are not showing God's love for that person. You are acting as if they and their feelings are worthless and unimportant to God.

Jesus tells us that "others will know that we are Christians by our love for one another" (John 13:35).

God wants you to show kindness to everyone. In the Bible we find " . . . blessed is he who is kind to the needy . . . . whoever is kind to the needy honors God" (Prov. 14:21,31). Remember that the ones who are rejected by others are in the greatest need of your kindness.

Maybe you agree with your friends. The person they reject is also your enemy because he or she has been unkind to you. In that case, you must trust that God will handle their attitude or action. They are responsible to God, not you. Your responsibility is to love them. When that seems impossible, remember God promises His love to enable you to:

> love your enemies, to be good to them, and lend to them without expecting to get anything back. Then your reward will be great, and you will be sons of the Most High, because he is kind to the ungrateful and wicked. Be merciful, just as your Father is merciful" (Luke 5:35-36).

Acting with godly kindness is always the right thing to do, and He will give you the power to do it, if you ask.

Additional Verses

1. "Make sure that nobody pays back wrong for wrong, but always try to be kind to each other and to everyone else" (1 Thess. 5:15).

2. "And the Lord's servant must not quarrel; instead, he must be kind to everyone, able to teach, not resentful" (2 Tim. 2:24).

3. "Be kind and compassionate to one another, forgiving each other, just as in Christ God forgave you" (Eph. 4:32).

Implications for the Older Child

Joy smiled broadly as she entered my seventh-grade homeroom. Her excitement and anticipation seemed to energize her sparkling blue eyes and gleaming auburn hair. New to the school, she reached out to others with happy enthusiasm. But her happiness was short-lived.

Being from another state, speaking with a different accent, and being the lone redhead in the class, she was ostracized and harassed by the other students. It seemed that they were intent on breaking her spirit. Finally one brave girl, herself a former outcast, befriended her and helped her to withstand the unpleasant attacks of the others.

Why were these young people so cruel? Many came from Christian homes and attended church each week. As a teacher, I've observed that teenagers are constantly accepting and rejecting each other in an attempt to break away from the influence of their parents and find acceptance from their peers. Cruelty results when anyone who is slightly different may feel the brunt of their attacks.

Knowing that this type of behavior is typical of early teens who are attempting to break away from the influence of their parents and find acceptance by their peers, Christian parents can help their child develop a lifelong value system that applies God's Word and wisdom in their personal relationships.

Wisdom comes from God (Jas. 3:17) and is shown by the kind of life we live. The Bible tells us wisdom from heaven is first of all pure, then peace-loving, considerate, submissive, full of mercy and good fruit, impartial, and sincere.

In the effort to cultivate a mature attitude, one that is positive rather than negative, it is essential to encourage your child to study God's Word and identify the attitudes He desires.

When your child is tempted to use the judgments of his

peers as the source of his friendships, encourage him or her to identify the reasons a child is being rejected, to ask if they are legitimate or based on prejudice and gossip. Ask him what God's Word says about his attitudes towards others. Encourage him to evaluate a relationship and not to react impulsively.

Remind your child that we are all special, created in God's likeness (2 Cor. 3:18), that each person has value. By behaving as children of God, we have the privilege of choosing our friends based on Christian love and a knowledge of God's guidance and directives.

12

Some of My Friends Talk Back, Yell, or Make Fun of Their Parents. No One Says It's Wrong. How Does God Want Me to Treat My Parents?

Adult Response

Parents are a special gift from God. We are to show you His love, care for your needs, and help you make good decisions so your actions will be right. Because we are God's gift to you, it is very important that you love and respect us.

In Ephesians 6:1-3 God tells you, "Children, obey your parents in the Lord, for this is right. 'Honor your father and your mother'—which is the first commandment with a promise—'that it may go well with you and that you may enjoy long life on the earth.' "

God promises that if you obey and honor us, by not doing as other children do—making fun, talking back, or yelling at us—He will bless you and cause things to go well with you.

Show us the same love and respect you want us to show

you and God will reward you. You will be a witness to
your friends and pleasing to God. God says, "Children,
obey your parents in everything, for this pleases the
Lord." (Col. 3:20).

Additional Verses

1. "Each of you must respect his mother and father, . . .
I am the Lord your God" (Lev. 19:3).

2. "My son, keep your father's commands and do not
forsake your mother's teaching. Bind them upon your
heart forever; fasten them around your neck. When you
walk, they will guide you; when you sleep, they will watch
over you; when you awake, they will speak to you" (Prov.
6:20-22).

3. "A wise son heeds his father's instruction, but a
mocker does not listen to rebuke" (Prov. 13:1).

4. "A fool spurns his father's discipline, but whoever
heeds correction shows prudence" (Prov. 15:5).

Further Insights

In *The Strong-Willed Child*, James Dobson writes,

One of the most serious casualties in a permissive society
is the failure to connect behavior and consequences. Too
often, a three-year-old child screams insults at his mother,
but Mom stares blinking her eyes in confusion. . . . all
through childhood, loving parents seem determined to intervene between behavior and consequences, breaking the
connection and preventing the valuable learning that
could have occurred.

He adds, "The best approach is to expect boys and girls
to carry the responsibility that is appropriate for their
age, and occasionally to taste the bitter fruit that irre-
sponsibility bears."[5]

Gladys M. Hunt, in *Focus on Family Life*, advises,

Go to God regularly for help and wisdom. Then act confidently, with a strong note of certainty. He who hesitates finds reluctant obedience. Pray daily that your children's hearts will be available to the promptings of the Holy Spirit.[6]

Implications for the Older Child

Since the teen years signal a time for the child to become more independent of parental control, some revert to negative behavior. Seeing their friends' insolence, they may think this is the method of getting the upper hand, of showing their mother or father that adults are no longer in control.

Yet this is a time when children need greater direction in developing their value system. As a parent you have not only the right but the obligation to identify good and bad behavior. Yet you want to do that without estranging your young teenager. How is it done?

One church leader suggests, "Do not make hostile comments such as 'Don't do that because I say so' or 'I'm your parent and until you leave this home, I'll be the one to make decisions and I demand respect.'" Respect can be expected but seldom demanded.

You can begin by trying to establish and identify the reason your child's attitude has changed. Has he entered a new school and or made new friends? Is he having difficulty in his relationships in school? in his studies? Has your attitude changed? Are you becoming too critical of this difficult teenager? Are you too demanding?

By establishing communication, you can define the conflict. Remember that overpermissive parents as well as overprotective ones rob their children of the authority figure they admire and emulate. To earn the respect of your child, try to be sensitive to his needs, insecurities, and especially his desire to be accepted by his peers. Talk about these things openly and listen with interest to his fears, confusion, and questions.

Remember that youths are in transition from family associations to an ever-increasing variety of relationships with many people. As a parent you have the right to meet your child's friends and to let your son or daughter know you find certain behavior, such as insolence, unacceptable.

Encourage him/her in right choices of behavior and friendships. Help him see the possible consequences of objectionable behavior and guide him to recognize the benefits of making good choices in his friendships.

13

When Someone Hurts My Feelings, I Want to Hurt Them, Too. Why Should I Forgive Them? Why Can't I Just Stay Away from Them?

Tears streamed down Amy's face as she pushed open the front door. She ran to her bedroom and flung herself, sobbing, on the bed.

"Amy. I'm home," her dad called. "I left work early this afternoon, Honey. How was your day?" She heard his concerned voice as he searched for her.

Amy choked back the sobs. "Here I am, Daddy."

"Darling, what's wrong? Why are you crying?"

Through tears, Amy tried to explain. "Oh, Dad, Sandra passed a note around the class to all the kids today, It said I had a big nose. Everybody laughed. When the note got to me, I wanted to die right there. Sandra is so mean. I don't know why she hates me so much."

Amy pushed her face back into the damp folds of her pillow. "I'm never going to speak to her again," she mumbled.

Her muffled words touched her father's heart. He placed his hand on her shoulder and gently patted.

Amy turned to look at him. "Daddy, when Sandra hurt my feelings today, I wanted to get back at her—hurt her, too—see how she'd like someone treating her like that."

With another quiet sob, she asked, "Do I have to forgive her? Can't I just stay away from her, ignore her?"

Adult Response

When someone hurts us, it is our natural human reaction to want to return the hurt, but this is wrong. It's sin. When Adam and Eve disobeyed God in the Garden of Eden, they caused sin to enter our lives. Each one of us is born with a natural tendency to sin. God could not look at sin or have a relationship with us until that sin was forgiven and removed. Jesus made that possible.

When Jesus came to live with us on earth, He showed us a better way— a way that helps us as well as the person who has hurt us. This way is through forgiveness. The Bible teaches us that, "The wages of sin are death"(Rom 6:23). Only Jesus, God's Son could live a perfect life and die on the cross to pay the penalty for our sin.

His death and blood cover our sin and allow us to be forgiven and have a relationship with God. Jesus forgave us first. On the cross, He said, "Father, forgive them for they know not what they do" (Luke 23:34, KJV). The people who killed Jesus, hurt Him, but He still forgave them. We, too, must forgive those who hurt us. God gives us the power to do this. ". . . forgiving each other just as in Christ, God forgave you" (Eph. 4:32).

Jesus' example and the Holy Spirit's power working in our hearts help us to forgive others.

Additional Verses

1. "Then I acknowledged my sin to you and did not cover up my iniquity. I said, 'I will confess my transgressions

to the Lord'—and you forgave the guilt of my sin" (Ps. 32:5).

2. "For I will forgive their wickedness and will remember their sins no more" (Heb. 8:12).

3. "If we confess our sins, he is faithful and just and will forgive us our sins and purify us from all unrighteousness" (1 John 1:9).

4. "When you were dead in your sins and in the uncircumcision of your sinful nature, God made you alive with Christ. He forgives us all our sins . . . triumphing over them by the cross" (Col. 2:13,15).

Implications for the Older Child

Apparently Jesus expected us to have difficulties with others (Matt. 5:39-44). He tells us we will have enemies and that there will be trouble. Our response? We are to turn the other cheek and love our assailant. That's not always easy—especially for a teenager.

Christian teenagers will be hurt. Under adverse peer pressure they may be ridiculed, mocked, and ostracized. Yet at times they misunderstand and highlight a stray word or comment meant in jest. The false message can lead to a feeling of complete rejection. What can parents do to help their child withstand these trials and prevent his becoming bitter and unhappy?

Ann Cannon writes in *Junior High Ministry* that in times like these parents can help their young teen apply the decision-making process to solve his/her problem. Ask him to relate the exact circumstances leading to the problem. Talk about any possible misconceptions or other reasons he may have misunderstood the other child's message.

Then help him to decide on a responsible response rather than reacting negatively. Remind your teen that we don't express God's love based on our feelings but on our will to follow in His footsteps. We choose to obey God's

Word and love others by the Holy Spirit's power, trusting God to determine the outcome according to His purposes.

Encourage your child to follow the example of Jesus who considered it important to restore relationships (Matt. 5:21-26; 18:21-35). Remind him that a Christian's love is different from the world's and that it's worth the risk involved to forgive and reach out to someone who has hurt him. It's not necessary to feel loving to forgive although that is often the result.

14

My Parents Are Divorced and My Dad (Mom) Doesn't Live with Us Anymore. Sometimes I Feel As If It Were All My Fault, and My Dad (Mom) Doesn't Love Me. How Can God Help Me?

Andrew remembered the times he hid on the stairs to listen to his parents' arguing. His auburn hair matted against his tear-streaked face, he huddled closer and closer to the stair rails, his eyes closed.

He hated those times when his parents, thinking he was fast asleep, shouted mean things to each other. He hated hearing his mother's sobs. They didn't know that he tiptoed down the stairs consumed with curiosity and plagued with fear. Night after night, argument after argument. Then they began using the awful word.

Divorce. It was all so frightening. He'd slip up the stairs to his room and snuggle into a tight ball beneath the comforter and pray that things would be right again. Finally, he'd fall asleep. Then it happened. His dad left.

One afternoon while staying with his grandmother, his mind seemed to be exploding with questions and doubts.

"Grandma," he finally whispered. "Now that Dad's gone, sometimes I feel it was my fault Mom and Dad got a divorce. I wonder if Dad still loves me. How can God love me if I caused it all?

Adult Response

Your dad and mother both love you. Sometimes two people don't get along well. They have a hard time loving each other. And sadly sometimes they aren't able to solve their disagreements and they divorce. You must remember it is their problem, and they alone must work it out. You didn't cause the separation of your mother and father.

God, your Heavenly Father, promises in His Bible that He will always be your Father and will never leave you. "Do not be afraid or discouraged, for the Lord God, My God is with you. He will not fail you or forsake you." These are David's words to his son Solomon (1 Chron. 28:20).

Realize that in every relationship we make mistakes and need God's forgiveness. Even if you have been wrong, God loves you and will never stop loving you. Ask God to forgive you for any sin you may have committed concerning your parents. If there were times when you said things you didn't mean; times when you disobeyed or were disrespectful, ask God to forgive you.

Then accept His forgiveness and the clean heart He promises in His Bible: "Though your sins are like scarlet, they shall be as white as snow; though they are red as crimson, they shall be like wool" (Isa. 1:18).

Although you need God's forgiveness for the mistakes you made, this does not mean you are the cause of your parents' divorce or that God doesn't love you. Always remember that both of your parents need your love. You are their child and they love you. Accept God's forgiveness and pray for your parents and for the solution to their problems.

Additional Verses

1. "Praise be to the God and Father of our Lord Jesus Christ, the Father of compassion and the God of all comfort, who comforts us in all our troubles" (2 Cor. 1:3).

2. "How great is the love the Father has lavished on us, that we should be called children of God!" (1 John 3:1).

3. "Though my father and mother forsake me, the Lord will receive me" (Ps. 27:10).

4. "You, O Lord, are our Father" (Isa. 63:16).

Further Insights

Tim LaHaye, in *The Battle for the Family*, says,

> I am convinced that death is easier for a child to handle than divorce. When my father died, I experienced traumatic grief for a while. But even at ten years of age I could understand that my thirty-four-year-old father could suddenly die from a heart attack, without rejecting me as a person. I often consoled myself with the thought, If dad had a choice, he would be with us.
> The child of divorce has no such means of assurance.[7]

LaHaye predicts that current divorce practices will result in a whole generation of "psychologically wounded adults" incapable of giving selfless love.

Writing on the effect of divorce on children, Roger Allen and Ron Rose say in *Common Sense Discipline*, "If both natural parents are around, children have to learn to live in two different homes. Sometimes parents will use the kids as weapons to get back at their ex."[8] This should be avoided at all costs. Children cannot withstand the emotional turmoil of choosing sides, and it may increase their sense of guilt.

Implications for the Older Child

Recent statistics suggest that by the year 2000, half of all children in the nation will have lived through a divorce before reaching the age of eighteen. Theorists submit many causes for divorces and the increasing threats to marriages, but the effect on children in the family must be addressed as well.

Allen J. Schwartzberg, an adolescent psychiatrist, maintains that teenagers feel angry, fearful, depressed, and guilty when faced with divorce. Divorce changes their way of living significantly. The loss of continuity and structure in their lives proves to be destructive to their growing self-image and inherent need for stability.

One of the top fears of all teenagers is the breakup of the family. To a teenager who knows God's plan for the permanence of marriage, a divorce can be traumatic. Yet most ministers and church members recognize that divorce happens, and they also acknowledge that God forgives the repentant.

If discussing divorce plans with your teenager, acknowledge your own feelings of anger, disappointment, and rejection. Search out verses of comfort in God's Word for both of you as you anticipate the new life-style. A teen is capable of understanding and envisioning life with a single parent. Yet this often doesn't prevent his angry rejection of his parents. Dejected and ashamed, he may avoid his friends as well. Patience and consistent love can bring gradual healing and help remove any relationship gap that may exist.

David Elkind says (in *Focus on the Family* magazine for April 1985):
"Teenagers are not adults capable of carrying the adult responsibilities we confer upon them." He adds that the imposition of premature adulthood can impair a teen's ability to build a secure self-image and/or may lead to adult-like stress.

Despite the closeness that may result between the two, teenager and parent, a parent must guard against developing a destructive dependency on the child. Assure him that the disagreement and breakup is between the parents and is not the teenager's fault.

As you talk with your teenager, listen to his concerns, assure him of both parents' love and desire for his happiness, of God's love and desire to forgive His people, and strengthen his sense of being capable of handling the situation with God's power. Again assure him that he can depend on the Lord to help him deal with the difficult adjustments ahead.

15

At Times I Feel Like Doing Things I've Been Told Not to Do. Why Is It Wrong to Do Something as Long as No One Knows and It Isn't Hurting Anyone Else?

Michael noticed the note tucked between the pages of his math book. He quickly removed it and hid it in his lap, slowly unfolding the creases. He scanned its contents.

Hi, Michael,

Let's go to the pond tomorrow afternoon. You tell your mom you're at my house. I'll tell my mom we're at your house. Then we can sneak away and fish. There aren't any snakes out there like your mom said. You're not going to chicken out, are you? Come on; let's go. It'll be fun.

Tom

Michael carefully refolded the paper and stuck it in his pocket. He knew note passing was against the rules. Besides he sure didn't want Mrs. Lincoln to find *this* note and read it.

He felt Tom's stare from across the room, but he resisted the urge to look at him. What was he going to do? He didn't want to be accused of being a wimp but his mom had told him to stay away from the pond. One child had already died from a snakebite. But that was two years ago. *Those snakes are sure to be gone by now with all the building going on nearby,* he reasoned. Tom was one of the most popular kids in school. If Tom made fun of him, he'd never live it down.

The rest of the day passed in a blur. Michael grew more miserable every minute. What was he going to do?

Arriving home, his mom greeted him cheerfully. "Hi, Son, what happened interesting today?"

"Nothing much," Michael said.

"Did you do well on your Math test?"

"OK, I guess."

Michael hesitated, then said, "Mom, what do you do if someone asks you to do something you know is wrong, and you're afraid all the kids will call you 'chicken' if you don't do it?"

Adult Response

By doing something we know is wrong, we are going against our desire to live a life that pleases God. Even if no other person on earth knows what we are doing, God knows. When you become a Christian, you belong to God's Son, Jesus Christ. He wants you to follow His Son's example. Our whole lives are lived before God and with Him. Paul wrote to the Philippians, "Whatever happens, conduct yourselves in a manner worthy of the gospel of Christ" (Phil. 1:27).

He also wrote "So whether you eat or drink or whatever you do, do it all for the glory of God" (1 Cor. 10:31). Every moment of the day, your behavior matters to God. He loves you and because you love Him, you should want to act in a way pleasing to Him.

It's important, too, because when you do what is right, you have a clear conscience before God, giving you peace of mind. "Dear friends," the apostle John wrote, "if our hearts do not condemn us, we have confidence before God and receive from him anything we ask because we obey his commands and do what pleases him" (1 John 3:21).

When we seek to obey God's will and do the things that please Him, we don't have to live with a guilty conscience, worried that someone will discover our hidden wrongdoing. We are free of guilt. Pleasing God as He watches over us each day and a clear conscience are well worth saying "no" to our friends when we are tempted to do the wrong thing.

And don't forget, God cares about you always. He is concerned about the things you do. He's your best friend, and He will only encourage you to do things that will prove to be good for your life. Don't let your best friend down.

Additional Verses

1. "Nothing in all creation is hidden from God's sight. Everything is uncovered and laid bare before the eyes of him to whom we must give account" (Heb. 4:13).

2. "For the eyes of the Lord are on the righteous and his ears are attentive to their prayer, but the face of the Lord is against those who do evil" (1 Pet. 3:12).

3. "For the eyes of the Lord range throughout the earth to strengthen those whose hearts are fully committed to him" (2 Chron. 16:9).

4. "Do not conform any longer to the pattern of this world, but be transformed by the renewing of your mind. Then you will be able to test and approve what God's will is—his good, pleasing and perfect will" (Rom. 12:2).

Further Insights

"Right vs. wrong: a child meets the two categories early in life. He's expected to choose one, reject the other. And he sincerely wants to (most of the time). But how?"[9] ask

Dean and Grace Merrill in *Together at Home*. They suggest that parents (1) think what Jesus would do; (2) think of the results; (3) pray for help; (4) know or find out what the Bible says about the subject; and (5) talk with other parents, pastors, or leaders.

In *Values Begin at Home,* Ted Ward says,

> Since every human must take those first steps of discovery to find right and wrong, the relationship with parents is crucial. If parents are doing as God intended, they are providing consistent clues about what is right and what is wrong. The child reaches out, explores, and receives the clues that are needed. Those clues must be reliable.
>
> The earliest awareness of moral conscience is simple: some things are right and some are wrong. The child's moral sense is thus developed. It is important that the child's relationship with the major source of those clues, the parents, be filled with respect and love.[10]

Implications for the Older Child

The teenage years could be called "the age of rebellion." For some it is short-lived. For others it takes many years of hard knocks for growth to occur. What is a Christian parent to do when faced with teenage peer pressures that may include drugs, illicit sex, rejection, and even unwanted pregnancy?

First, remember that you are not alone with your problem. Pray and depend on God's promises. There is much you can do to help your child say "no" when faced with the temptations of peer pressure.

Start by being loving, compassionate, and understanding. Keep communication open. Be ready to listen when your preteen child comes to you with concerns. To ridicule or negate the problem even though it may seem insignificant to you is to drive a wedge in your relationship. A bad haircut, unshaved legs, poor grades, or lack of a date for a teenager can be a traumatic situation. Respect your adolescent's thoughts and feelings. Be sympathetic and understanding.

By maintaining communication throughout your child's early years, you are keeping the door open when adolescent isolation becomes apparent. Stuart Alan Capons in *The Parents' Guide to Teenagers* warns however, "Don't insist on intimacy. If your adolescent child will not talk with you, perhaps you can find another adult-teacher, minister or relative to discuss personal matters."[11] Choose someone whose opinion you respect and who may have a greater influence on your child's ability to make choices about rejecting negative peer pressures.

Above all, honor your teenager's need for privacy. It's important for him/her to have his/her own room, possessions, private thoughts, mail, phone calls, and diaries untouched by others. To ignore this need is to ask for anger, insults, and complaints. Display trust in your child's ability to make responsible decisions. Compliment him/her when good choices are made.

Maintain parental control, set limits and enforce them. All children need the security of knowing the parent is in charge even though he may object, complain, and fight the restrictions. Firm discipline now will help him develop the inner control he will need throughout life.

Try throughout these critical years to help your child develop a strong self-image, giving him the confidence to face the opposing views of others. Compliment him when he succeeds, help him to see himself as unique and special in God's eyes even when he is feeling threatened and afraid, when he thinks of himself as insignificant and unloved.

Try to maintain a positive attitude. Throughout this period in your child's life, hang on to your own sense of humor. Always remember that "this, too, will pass." Most Christian teens come through these years unharmed and with a deeper respect for their parents. Take time to enjoy your child and the positive results of his well-made decisions.

16
Does God Care If I Lie or Use Bad Words?

"Andy, did you finish your homework?"

"Sure, Mom," Andy said, turning the TV volume down in his bedroom so she wouldn't hear it.

Homework! I hate homework! No, I haven't quite finished it yet, but I'm almost done. Anyway, I can do it later. I'm sure not going to miss my favorite program to do homework.

The evening passed. Television show after show came and went. Time to go to bed and Andy still hadn't finished his homework. Actually, he forgot all about it until 2:00 p.m. the next day when Mrs. Carlson asked the class to turn in their completed homework. Otherwise, they'd receive a zero for the day.

Andy gulped. *A zero!* He'd already gotten several for incomplete work. Mrs. Carlson had warned him that if he got one more zero, she'd call his mother. Oh, no. His stomach tightened. His mom would know about the zero.

After school, he heard his mother's voice as he approached the back door. "Mrs. Carlson. How are you?" He hurried to his room, thinking, *Now I'm in for it.* Moments later he heard his mother's slow, steady footsteps on the stairs.

"Andy, are you in your room?"

"Yes, Mom."

"I think you know we need to talk, Son," he heard.

"Yes, ma'am."

"Mrs. Carlson just called. I guess you know what she wanted to talk about."

"Yes, ma'am."

His mother's voice was calm and determined. "I'm disappointed in that zero you received for not completing your homework, Andy. Something else troubles me more, however."

With a questioning look, Andy glanced at his mother.

"I'm most upset by the fact you lied to me. You told me you had finished your homework."

"But Mom, I was almost finished." Andy's voice trailed off.

"Andy, lying is a serious problem. Both God and I consider it extremely serious. Have you ever wondered what God thinks about lying?"

"No, Mom. I'm sorry I lied to you. I really thought I'd finish my homework in time." He paused. "Does God really care about lying? Is it in the Bible?"

Adult Response

The Bible is clear that God hates lies. Lying directly opposes everything God is because God *is* Truth. Jesus tells us, "I am the way and the *truth* and the life" (John 14:6). He says, "I tell you the truth" more than sixty times in the New Testament because He is truth and always tells the truth.

When we belong to Jesus Christ, we represent Him. We must be truthful in everything if we are to be good representatives. Hebrew 6:18 tells us, "It is impossible for God to lie." John says, "No lie comes from the truth" (1 John 2:21).

Because God is truth and our words do matter, we should never lie. If you do, you need to ask God's forgiveness. And choose not to do it again. We may think lying is unimportant, but it is very important to God and causes us a lot of problems. If we continue lying, small lies may turn into big ones. We tend to create bigger lies to hide the small ones. Soon we may be unable to separate the truth from lies. Besides living with the fear of being caught, we learn that no one trusts a liar.

God tells us in the Bible that words are very important to Him. Even God's son Jesus is called the "Word of life" (1 John 1:1). We learn that our words tell others what is in our heart (Rev. 19:13). A heart that belongs to Jesus is clean and pure and this will be shown through our words. Lies are distorted truth.

Additional Verses

1. "Whoever of you loves life and desires to see many good days, keep your tongue from evil and your lips from speaking lies" (Ps. 34:12-13).

2. "Keep falsehood and lies far from me; give me neither poverty nor riches, but give me only my daily bread" (Prov. 30:8).

3. "But now you must rid yourselves of all such things as these: anger, rage, malice, slander, and filthy language from your lips. Do not lie to each other since you have taken off your old self with its practices and have put on the new self, which is being renewed in knowledge in the image of its Creator" (Col. 3:8-10).

Further Insights

Paul Lewis says,

> If your child has developed a clear understanding of honesty rooted in Scripture, he or she will rise above the frequent trap of seeing right and wrong only in terms of what is most pleasurable, approved by others, or most expedient. The child's conscience will be sensitive to dishonesty in all its forms and will help him or her consistently avoid it.[12]

Also "Lying is a signal to stop and spend some quality one-on-one time with your child,"[13] say Roger Allen and

Ron Rose. They suggest a parent remind the child that life is better when we tell the truth. Then, we don't have to face the consequences of our actions which only worsens the situation.

Lying can become a habitual problem during elementary school years unless parents take decisive action early. Children tell lies for several reasons. Sometimes they feel like they have to invent things so people will listen to them. Sometimes the child is just trying to protect himself from severe punishment.

In any case, consistent parental intervention can prevent habitual lying and train the child to speak truthfully.

Implications for the Older Child

Urie Branfenbrenner, eminent authority on child development at Cornell University is quoted as saying,

> . . . the peer group tends to undermine adult socialization efforts and to encourage egocentrism, aggression and antisocial behavior. A large scale survey of American sixth graders found that those children who were most peer-oriented were also those who reported engaging most often in antisocial activities such as lying to adults, smoking and using bad language.[14]

Profanity is something all children hear—on TV, in the movies, and even at home. It's often considered grown-up language. Young teens, striving to break away from parental control, may use profanity to appear "adult." For some teens, it is a special language—one they hide from their parents, teachers, and church leaders.

When a parent is aware that the child is using profanity, it is his or her responsibility to challenge the use and to try to correct the behavior. You may not see an immediate change, but you, a Christian parent, have the authority and right to remind him of the biblical basis for refraining from the practice.

Gary Hunt tells of hearing one of his young church school students, a strong Christian raised in a Christian family, use a questionable word. When he rebuked him, the boy said, "I heard my brother say it and I tried it out on my dad and he didn't say anything."[15] It's well to remember, then, that in the eyes of a teenager, to ignore lying and profanity is to condone it.

Lying, too, is a concern to the parents of their teenage child. Oftentimes a parent should reflect on his or her own behavior. Do you tell lies for convenience? Research suggests that children who lie most often come from homes in which parents also lie or break rules.

Besides watching your own behavior, check on your child's friends. Children who lie often have friends who lie. At times, parents encourage teenagers to lie by being too judgmental and questioning. By respecting your child's privacy, you will try to limit questions to those that concern personal well-being, work habits, behavior away from home, and TV watching habits. Asking pointed questions about activities and friends may lead to sullen, evasive responses as well as outright lies.

Of course, a parent has the right to know who a child's friends are and what they do in their free time. Encouraging your child to invite friends into your home will often eliminate the need for questions. If you catch a friend in a lie or in some other antisocial behavior, point out the negative aspects of the behavior to your child. Promote new friends and activities.

Remember that a parent's trust may be the most important effect on his truthfulness. Psychiatrists say that parents who show their child that he or she is trusted make the child feel proud and grown-up. Too often we judge a teenager "guilty" without giving him or her a chance to defend himself. Remind your child that if he or she continues to lie, not only will you be forced to discipline, but the risk of losing your trust may result.

Paul Ekman points out that ultimately, mutual trust is the answer. "Trust your child with the truth and you will reap the rewards of honesty."[16]

17

Sometimes I Brag About Myself and My Family. Lately My Friends Have Been Avoiding Me. What Does God Think About Bragging and Being Proud?

Adult Response

Knowing God is more important than anything else in life. We cannot know God until we realize we need Him. He made us. He takes care of us each day. He provides our food, our clothes, and our homes. Anything we accomplish is because He has helped us do it. To succeed, we need God.

Because of these gifts from God, we have nothing to be proud of or boast about except to thank Him and tell others what great things God has done for us.

"Let him who boasts, boast about this: that he understands and knows me, that I am the Lord, who exercises kindness, justice and righteousness on earth, for in these I delight," declares the Lord (Jer. 9:24).

When we brag about ourselves, people usually think one of two things. First, they may think that we are looking down on their accomplishments and abilities as being less than ours. This, of course, hurts their feelings and makes them dislike us. No one wants to feel he is being "put down."

They may also think that we are unsure of ourselves and have to brag to prove we are worth noticing or liking. This, too, makes people dislike us and think less of us. Working so hard to get approval and prove ourselves by bragging is prideful, and our friends don't like bragging, prideful people.

God tells us in the Bible that everything we have comes from Him. This includes our relationship with Him. We are also told that we can do nothing ourselves to assure intelligence, beauty, or material things in our lives. "For it is by grace you have been saved, through faith—and this not from yourselves, it is a gift of God—not by works, so that no one can boast" (Eph. 2:8-9). Everything we have is a gift from God. If we do boast, it should be about God, giving thanks to Him for our blessings.

Additional Verses

1. "Let another praise you, and not your own mouth; someone else, and not your own lips" (Prov. 27:2).

2. "Not to us, O Lord, not to us but to your name be the glory, because of your love and faithfulness" (Ps. 115:1).

3. "But, 'Let him who boasts boast in the Lord.' For it is not the one who commends himself who is approved, but the one whom the Lord commends" (2 Cor. 10:17-18).

4. "Your boasting is not good" (1 Cor. 5:6).

5. "How can you believe if you accept praise from one another, yet make no effort to obtain the praise that comes from the only God?" (John 5:44)

Implications for the Older Child

Teenage boys are particularly competitive in both social and physical situations. They like to talk about their real and imagined exploits—to brag. Impressing their peers is the "name of the game."

Bragging is similar to lying and may result from a child's low self-esteem. Stephen Crott, in his pamphlet written for Christian athletes, "What Makes You Special?" talks about the human dilemma of choosing between two voices: God, who tells us we are precious, or Satan, who tells us we are worthless. Self-esteem emerges from the voice we hear and believe.

Although it may not eliminate all bragging, you can help your child develop a strong self-image by stressing the things which you admire about him or her. Remind him/her that each of the strengths is a gift from God. Also remind him that God considers each of us unique and has equipped us with talent (1 Cor. 12:15), with the desire to accomplish our goals and with the energy to do it.

He has also equipped us with power to master our weaknesses. By depending on Him for guidance, we will be led to recognize our strengths and acknowledge our weaknesses, making bragging a wasted, unproductive effort.

18

I Know Passing Notes or Whispering About People in My Class Is Wrong, but Others Do It. What Does God Think of This?

Adult Response

Jesus Christ teaches us to love one another. God is love and He desires that others see His love in and through our actions and attitudes. This is the way we show other people we are Christians and are different. Jesus said, "A new commandment I give you. Love one another. As I have loved you, so you must love one another. By this all men will know that you are my disciples, if you love one another" (John 13:34-35).

When you criticize, make fun of, or hurt other children through notes and words, you are acting like the children who don't know God. You are not being loving or displaying God's love.

The Bible also teaches us not to harm others with our words or actions. They, too, are God's children and are precious to Him. If you feel they have a problem or need changing in their thoughts or actions, remember that no one is perfect. We, too, have faults and weaknesses. Jesus teaches us, "Do to others what you would have them do to you" (Matt. 7:12).

The next time you are passed a note or you hear a mean comment about someone, don't participate. Destroy the note or try to think of something nice about the person being ridiculed. Change the subject whenever possible. If you belong to Christ, be willing to be different from the crowd. His Holy Spirit will give you the power to show Christ's love.

Additional Verses

1. "You, then, why do you judge your brother? Or why do you look down on your brother? For we will all stand before God's judgment seat. So then each of us will give an account of himself to God" (Rom. 14:10,12).

2. "A perverse man stirs up dissension and a gossip separates close friends" (Prov. 16:28).

3. "But who are you to judge your neighbor?" (Jas. 4:11)

4. "Be kind and compassionate to one another, forgiving each other, just as in Christ God forgave you" (Eph. 4:32).

Further Insights

Gladys M. Hunt says, "Love involves friendship. It contains a quiet kind of appreciation and affection for another's spirit and intellect." She continues,

> It is important at the outset to realize that sin has set a tremendous road block in the way of our loving another person. Any hope we have of loving others is found in God. We love because He first loved us.[17]

Roger Allen and Ron Rose declare in *Common Sense Discipline,*

> Children learn a lot from watching others. Sometimes they learn from the strengths of others and sometimes from the weaknesses. We've all seen children trying to walk like their daddy. . . . Don't underestimate modeling as an effective communicator of love.[18]

Ted Ward writes,

> Christian values? One word says them all: LOVE. Love of God for people, love of the redeemed for God the Savior, and love of people for each other are the three basic kinds of love. The Bible shows the fulfillment that comes to those who love God. The Bible also shows that love for others is the natural outgrowth of God's love for us.[19]

Implications for the Older Child

One outstanding teenage characteristic is the desire to conform—to be an exact duplicate of all the other teens. He doesn't want to stand out in a crowd. Stop and look at a group of eighth or ninth graders. The girls' dresses are the same length and style; their hairstyles are similar; and their speech and mannerisms are identical. Proof can be found in the manufacturers' names attached to their designer jeans.

When a young person in a group of teens is different in any way, it may spur unfavorable comments and snickers from their peers. James Dobson tells of an incident in his own life. A new boy showed up in the Sunday School class he attended. Dobson observed that the boy's ears reminded him of jeep fenders.

He shared his observation with his friends in the class. They began to call the new boy "Jeep Fenders." At first the new boy ignored the comments, but finally he fled from the class and never returned. Dobson observed that this unchristian behavior was not premeditated or intended to hurt the child.

Yet it had never been explained that people are sensitive, that they dislike being teased, that there are certain areas of our life over which we have no control such as the shape of our ears. He hadn't been taught to respect and protect the feelings of others.

Parents and teachers have an obligation to acquaint their children with the important biblical lesson found in John 13:34-35. Jesus told his disciples, "A new commandment I give to you, that you love one another, even as I have loved you. . . . By this all men will know that you are my disciples, if you have love for one another"(NASB). To show the love of Jesus, adult teachers of teens should consider it a priority to teach respect for others.

19

Some Kids in School Take Pencils and Things from the Teacher's Desk. Other Friends Share Their Answers on Tests and Homework. Is This Really Wrong?

"Mom, may I ask Wendy over to spend the night on Friday?" Laura looked hopeful as she watched her mother knead the biscuit dough for their dinner. She sniffed deeply, savoring the aroma of pot roast.

"Who is Wendy, Laura? A school friend?"

"Yes," Laura said. "She's a new girl. We're in the same English class."

"What do you know about her? Is she a Christian?"

Laura stared at the pattern on the linoleum floor. "I'm not sure," she said. "She wears T-shirts with her church's name on the front. Yet last week, she got mad at me when I wouldn't show her my answers to the test questions."

Her mother looked up, surprised. Her blue eyes searched Laura's face. "Do you mean she tried to cheat from your paper? Well! Surely you could find another friend to invite over."

"Ah, Mom," Laura moaned. "Being Christian when others aren't is tough. Wendy only did it once. Why is that so wrong? Everyone else seems to cheat sometimes."

Adult Response

Cheating is wrong because, like stealing, it is taking something which doesn't belong to you. When you steal, you are taking someone else's property. When you cheat, you are stealing another person's idea.

Getting something dishonestly might seem OK temporarily. The person might get a better grade on one test. But he hasn't learned the material and finally his deceit will be discovered. Cheating is a form of lying, too. It is saying you know something that you don't. The Bible teaches us,

> There are six things the Lord hates, seven that are detestable to Him: haughty eyes, a *lying tongue*, hands that shed innocent blood, a heart that devises wicked schemes, feet that are quick to rush into evil, a *false witness who pours out lies* and a man who stirs up dissension among brothers (Prov. 6:16-19).

All falsehood, lies, and deceitfulness are against God

and His Word because God is always truthful and honest. He wants us to be truthful and honest Christians.

In David's prayer to God, he says, "I know, my God, that you test the heart and are pleased with integrity. All these things have I given willingly and with honest intent" (1 Chron. 29:17). The dictionary defines "honest" as "not given to lying, cheating, stealing, etc." Rejecting these things is the kind of life that pleases God and causes others to see Jesus Christ in us.

Additional Verses

1. "The Lord abhors dishonest scales, but accurate weights are his delight" (Prov. 11:1).

2. "Food gained by fraud tastes sweet to a man, but he ends up with a mouth full of gravel" (Prov. 20:17).

3. "He who has clean hands and a pure heart . . . will receive blessing from the Lord and vindication from God his Savior" (Ps. 24:4-5).

4. "The Lord detests lying lips, but he delights in men who are truthful" (Ps. 12:22).

Implications for the Older Child

Teenagers are often challenged to make moral decisions in their day-to-day school and church life. They may see their friends and classmates receive attention for good grades and behavior knowing that the person cheats and/or steals. In fact, at times peer cliques will make theft the criteria for acceptance.

Some insecure child may think, *So what? Everyone's doing it. I want to succeed, too. I want to be part of the popular crowd.*

A parent may be tempted at times to look away from a

seemingly insignificant incident and ignore a child's misbehavior. It's not easy to see your child suffer while others who are less honorable receive awards and acclamation. Your response unfortunately may lead your teen to think it's OK to cheat or steal if you aren't caught.

Billy Graham reminds young people, "After all, you must first please Him (Christ) and then other things will fall in line in due time."[20] By remembering the trauma of being out of contact with the Lord because of wrongdoing, remind your child that when we do things we know as Christians are wrong, we still have to deal with our conscience. Peace with God is impossible when we break His laws.

By being an example and encourager in making moral and ethical decisions, your own life can be the beacon light your child needs to guide him in these important choices.

20

When I See Something I Think Is Bad on TV, Does God Want Me to Turn It Off or Doesn't He Care?

The house was quiet. Everyone else was asleep when Ben flipped on Saturday morning cartoons. Eyes focused on the screen, he stared listlessly. Then the antics of cartoon characters grabbed his attention.

Sitting cross-legged around a coffee table, the characters started chanting strange, unintelligible sounds. A black-veiled woman in flowing robes slowly passed her hands over a crystal ball on the table. She muttered words he'd never heard before.

Suddenly uncomfortable, Ben squirmed in his seat. He knew something was wrong even though the screen showed only cartoon characters. The chanting and the woman's eerie voice seemed evil. *Why do I feel so funny*, he thought. *They're only cartoons. How can they be bad?*

Later, he questioned his mother. "Mom, I see things on TV I think are bad." He told her about the cartoon. "I thought cartoons were supposed to be funny. Is that all this was or should I have turned it off?"

Adult Response

What we see and hear goes into our minds and stays there, a permanent record. It affects the way we think, feel, and the way we live. God talks a lot about the use of the mind.

Paul tells us in Romans, "Do not conform any longer to the pattern of this world, but be transformed by the renewing of your mind" (Rom. 12:2). God wants us to be careful about the way we use our minds and what we think about. It matters to God. Paul also says: "Whatever is true, whatever is noble, whatever is right, whatever is pure, whatever is lovely, whatever is admirable—if anything is excellent or praiseworthy—think about such things" (Phil. 4:8).

The next time you watch a TV program or read a book, ask yourself, "Is this something God would want to be permanently stored in my brain? Is it something that fits the list of things God wants me to think about? If it doesn't fit these guidelines, choose to turn off the TV or put the book away.

Doing this will help you grow closer to God and show Him how much you love Him. Jesus says, "Whoever has my commands and obeys them, he is the one who loves me. He who loves me will be loved by my Father, and I too will love him and show myself to him" (John 14:21).

Additional Verses

1. "Love the Lord your God with all your heart and with all your heart and with all your soul and with all your might" (Deut. 6:5, NASB).

2. "Set your mind on things above, not on earthly things" (Col. 3:2).

3. "The mind of sinful man is death, but the mind controlled by the Spirit is life and peace" (Rom. 8:6).

4. "You were taught,... to be made new in the attitude of your minds; and to put on the new self, created to be like God in true righteousness and holiness" (Eph. 4:22-24).

Implications for the Older Child

When handling the problem of TV-watching, parents may overlook an opportunity to strengthen important Christian values. Television is so much a part of contemporary life it's almost like another member of the family. And its effect can be either good or bad. Children develop lifelong values often based simply on cartoon characters, popular situation-comedy figures, and horror-movie villains.

It is said all our lives are governed by one or more general themes, directions, goals, objectives, or values. Psychiatrist Gordon W. Allport writes, "a sense of direction and a clearly focused value system is the mark of a mature person."[21] Christians have an overriding value that supersedes all others—the love of Christ and the desire to follow in His footsteps.

With this example, Christian parents can be undergirded in their effort to control the amount and quality of TV their teenagers watch. Because you can't constantly monitor your child's viewing, strive to help him/her develop a sense of good, bad, right, and wrong.

One parent succeeded in doing this by watching his

son's favorite program with him. Afterwards, they discussed the moral implications of the dominant message. They talked about how Jesus might have reacted if He had watched the program with them. Then they opened the Bible and searched for guidance.

By talking with your teenager about your reasons for encouraging him to become more selective in TV-watching, you can help him or her become an intelligent viewer. Some of the questionable TV messages you can discuss include:

1. the existence of hidden messages concerning the use of alcohol and drugs, sex, crime, etc.

2. whether the main character's life-style and personal values are ones your child would want to emulate. Why or why not?

3. the educational value, truthfulness, bias, or language in the program.

4. whether the program strengthens American family life or degrades it, remember that recent surveys show that over 80 percent of Americans believe in God and many attend a church of worship.

5. the subliminal messages in music and popular comedies. Talk about how the brain stores both good and bad information and consider the possibility of incorrect words and messages rising to conscious thought at a later time to confuse and frighten.

Section III
Does the Way I Think Matter to God?
Questions About Attitudes

Section III
Does the Way I Think Matter to God?
Questions About Attitudes

As a child matures, thinking processes change significantly. In early childhood "concrete" thinking is evident. The child accepts all words at face value with little ability to interpret. This was graphically illustrated recently as I listened to my husband's Sunday sermon for children.

Telephone in hand, he asked the children if they knew their telephone numbers. Little hands waved in the air as they were called upon to recite their number. He dialed several of the numbers and found no one home, as anticipated. He then talked about busy signals. He explained that when we call to talk to God in prayer, we never get a busy signal. God is always available and ready to listen and talk with us.

Laura, a bouncy, brown-eyed four-year-old raised her hand. Puzzled, she asked, "How can I call God? I don't know His telephone number."

As adolescence approaches, thinking changes. Abstract concepts are explored and understood. As the teenager attempts to apply concrete ideas to a variety of circumstances, he may begin questioning and challenging these ideas as he searches for answers to the question, Is this concrete idea true in every circumstance? Inconsistencies may suddenly surface for the youth. We must be willing acknowledge these inconsistencies and seek to correct them.

A college student was discussing one of these inconsistencies with me last week. He is attending a Christian college where dancing is forbidden on campus. Yet, annually the school administration sponsors an off-campus school dance.

The inconsistency troubled the boy. "How can they say dancing is biblically wrong and then make it acceptable off-campus? This infers biblical truth is OK for some parts of life but irrelevant to others. There seems to be a lack of integration of biblical truth to life experiences. If we love God and believe His Bible, He should be influencing every aspect of life."

As parents, we can demonstrate our desire to conform our thinking to God's Word and respond with biblically consistent attitudes. Rather than rigidly holding to cultural and traditional views that may not be accurate according to the Bible, we can be open to changes that reflect biblical truth. Otherwise the teenager may become disillusioned and lose respect for us because of our unwillingness to "practice what we preach."

With growth, children's attitudes and actions will begin to reflect accurate application of biblical truth and a strong, mature individual will emerge. There will be joy in knowing that his framework of biblical values and principles will remain secure in the face of approaching adulthood.

21

When I Make a Decision, Why Should I Wait for God to Show Me What to Do? Can't I Do It My Way?

Adult Response

God has specific plans for your life. He created you to know Him and bring Him glory on earth by fulfilling His plans for you. By fulfilling God's plans and purposes for you, you will find true joy. The Lord told Jeremiah to tell the exiles, " 'I know the plans I have for you,' declares the Lord, 'plans to prosper you and not to harm you, plans to give you hope and a future' " (Jer. 29:11). God has hope and a future for you, too.

It should be your desire each day to find God's will for that day. We have Jesus' example. "For I have come down from heaven not to do my will but to do the will of him who sent me" (John 6:38). When Jesus completed His life on earth He could say, "I have brought you glory on earth by completing the work you gave me to do" (John 17:4).

We learn from Paul's Letter to the Ephesians, "We are God's workmanship, created in Christ Jesus to do good works, which God prepared in advance for us to do" (Eph. 2:10). God is very kind in giving us the tools to know and do His will.

As you faithfully read God's Word each day and pray to know what God's will is, He will show you. He promises: "If any of you lacks wisdom, he should ask God, who gives generously to all without finding fault, and it will be given to him" (Jas. 1:5). We find clear directions in Paul's Letter to the Romans,

I urge you, brothers, in view of God's mercy, to offer your bodies as living sacrifices. . . . Do not conform any longer to the pattern of this world, but be transformed by the renewing of your mind. Then you will be able to test and approve what God's will is—his good, pleasing and perfect will (Rom. 12:1-2).

You can discover God's will by giving your life completely to Him and choosing Christ's values and practices instead of the world's. Pray, asking God to "equip you with everything good for doing his will" (Heb. 13:21). He will answer your prayers because it is God's desire that you know His will and do it. Then your life will glorify, honor, and bring praise to Him.

Additional Verses

1. "Your kingdom come, your will be done on earth as it is in heaven" (Matt. 6:10).
2. "I desire to do your will, O my God; your law is within my heart" (Ps. 40:8).
3. "Teach me to do your will, for you are my God; may your good Spirit lead me on level ground" (Ps. 143:10).
4. "For it is God who works in you to will according to his good purposes" (Phil. 2:13).
5. "Instead, you ought to say, 'If it is the Lord's will, we will live and do this or that' " (Jas. 4:15).

Further Insights

In *Values Begin at Home*, Ted Ward says,

Obedience to God's Word and to God's will is very important. The Christian knows that a life of morality depends on obedience. Since what is moral is defined by the principles of God's Law, obedience to God's Law (or to the principles of the Law) is the way of morality and moral life. When Jesus said, "I am the way" (John 14:6), He was referring, in part to the life of obedience.[1]

Implications for the Older Child

Decisions, decisions. God gave us freedom to choose and choices by young people are increasingly more difficult to make in our changing society. Parents and other adults working with them realize that anxiety over choices is a major problem as they face pressure from peers, adults, and the world. It is encouraging to know that God has a plan for each life.

Most parents are intensely concerned over the possibility their children may make a serious error in judgment as they face choices concerning their future, vocation, marriage partner, and direction in life. We can all remember vividly our own poor choices and the dramatic effects they may have had on our lives. So how do you, a Christian parent, counsel your child?

1. Pray with him and for him that the Lord will show His will for him and give the guidance he needs so he will make the right choices and decisions.

2. Remind him that he can trust God's wisdom and encourage him to wait patiently as he seeks His will.

3. Lead him to the Bible for answers. Proverbs 3:5-6 tells us "Trust in the Lord with all your heart and lean not on your own understanding; in all your ways acknowledge him and he will make your paths straight."

4. To assist further, brainstorm options, look at the advantages and disadvantages of each choice. Help him to look at possible future outcomes of a decision. Ask, "How would that decision or choice affect you in three months? in a year? Would this decision be consistent with the direction God has already given you in His Word?"

5. Counsel that when we push ahead with our decisions without God's guidance we are showing a lack of trust in God, even contempt for God's will in our lives. God has specific plans and His promises help us discover them.

Philippians 2:13 reminds us that as we seek God's will, He will work out His plan through our lives.

22

It Seems Every Time I Want to Read a Book or Do Something I Enjoy, My Mother Gives Me a Job to Do. What Does God Think About Work and My Attitude About It?

Peter slouched deeper in the sofa cushions as he heard his mother call, "Peter, have you finished your afternoon chores?"

Eyes fixed on the Hardy Boy mystery, Peter held his breath. *If I don't answer, maybe she'll think I've gone out-side*, he thought.

"Peter, where are you?"

Shifting his weight slightly to move his cramped leg, he heard the sofa springs squeak.

Exasperated, his mother opened the den door, "Peter! You should answer me when I call. Have you finished picking up your room?"

Peter sighed. "Aw, Mom," he said. "This book is so good I can't put it down."

"You know that as members of a family, we all share the responsibility for our home. It's your job to clean your room before supper. Now run upstairs and finish the job. You've got fifteen minutes until we eat."

"OK, Mom," Peter said with a deep sigh. "But I don't have to like it," he mumbled as he trudged upstairs. "I'll bet God wouldn't care?"

Then he thought, *I wonder what He really does think about work and my attitude?*

Adult Response

Showing responsibility by helping with family chores is a part of growing up and maturing. God created work and He knows that it helps you find fulfillment in life. When you complete a task you feel successful. When you obey your parents and do God's will you please and glorify God and it also gives you a healthy outlook on your life.

Even God's creation tells us of God's work. Psalm 19 reads, "The heavens declare the glory of God; the skies proclaim the work of his hands" (v.1). God cares about the quality of your work. Paul says,

> Make it your ambition to lead a quiet life, to mind your own business and to work with your hands, just as we told you, so that your daily life may win the respect of outsiders and so that you will not be dependent on anybody (1 Thess. 4:11-12).

What makes the quality of our work pleasing to God? Your attitude makes the difference. If you grumble with discontent as you work, your work loses its value. God wants you to do your work according to His direction. The Bible tells us to work willingly with contentment, doing everything and completing the task lovingly for Jesus.

Colossians 3:23-24 teaches Christians,

> Whatever you do, work at it with all your heart, as working for the Lord, not for men since you know that you will receive an inheritance from the Lord as a reward. It is the Lord Christ you are serving.

The author of Hebrews says,

> God; . . . will not forget your work and love you have shown him as you have helped his people and continue to help them. We do not want you to become lazy, but to imitate those who through faith and patience inherit what has been promised (6:10,12).

The next time you're asked to do a job, do it for Jesus.

He *is* standing right there with you even if you can't see Him. By doing your work with a cheerful heart and attitude, you show Jesus that you love Him. "God loves a cheerful giver" (2 Cor. 9:7). Paul showed he learned that lesson when he wrote, "I have learned the secret of being content in any and every situation.... I can do everything through him who gives me strength" (Phil. 4:12-13).

Additional Verses

1. "All Scripture is God-breathed and is useful for teaching, rebuking, correcting and training in righteousness, so that the man of God may be thoroughly equipped for every good work" (2 Tim. 3:16-17).

2. "We were not idle when we were with you, nor did we eat anyone's food without paying for it. On the contrary we worked night and day, laboring and toiling so that we would not be a burden to any of you. We did this, ... in order to make ourselves a model for you to follow. For even when we were with you, we gave you this rule: 'If a man will not work, he shall not eat' " (2 Thess. 3:7-10).

3. "We work hard with our own hands" (1 Cor. 4:12).

Further Insights

Roger Allen and Ron Rose say,

Children are not genetically programmed to be responsible—they need training. A responsible child takes care of his room, his clothes, his possessions and himself .... He begins enjoying caring for others, too. [A responsible child] seems to be more and more aware that he is programmed for independence.[2]

Implications for the Older Child

Is there a teenager who doesn't try to avoid assigned duties, studies, or chores? Parents doubt it. Yet the Bible tells us to "Train up a child in the way he should go, Even when he is old, he will not depart from it" (Prov. 22:6, NASB).

Teaching children is hard work but the payoff is high and lasts a lifetime. An essential role of a parent is to help teenagers develop responsible work habits. To do this, definite tasks should be assigned at home and in school, chores that they are expected to perform satisfactorily. Explain that habits are energy efficient and that by doing chores automatically and habitually, habits will not only be reinforced, it will take less time to complete the chores.

Encourage your older teenager to seek part-time work for spending money and greater self-reliance. One of the major benefits a parent will observe is the increased sense of self-sufficiency and worth.

Teach your teenagers that:

• work is an integral part of life and we all need to be diligent in fulfilling our responsibilities.

• they should set goals and work quietly and systematically toward them.

• Christian volunteers who work through a desire to help others reap the benefits of showing Christ to their world.

• money has no lasting value in providing joy or building a good family life so don't use it as your prime criteria for work or living.

• criticism shouldn't be feared. Someone once said, "If you don't want to be criticized, don't say anything, don't do anything or be anything." Through criticism, we learn to accept responsibility for our actions and to improve our life and work.

23

My Friends Have Lots of Expensive Toys and Clothes. How Can I Be Thankful Rather than Jealous?

In the Bible, God says a lot about the things we own and our attitudes toward them. He tells us clearly that the most important things in life is to "Love the Lord your God with all your heart and with all your soul and with all your strength" (Deut. 6:5)

Television advertises cars, clothes, shoes, even toothpaste or soft drinks in such an appealing way that you begin to believe the advertisers. You start to think there is some value in the name of a product—as if the value of each person is determined by the product he uses or wears.

God doesn't measure a person's value by the things he or she has or buys. As a matter of fact, "things" matter little to God unless they can bring Him glory. Jesus told His disciples, "Therefore I tell you, do not worry about your life, what you will eat; or about your body, what you will wear. Life is more important than food, and the body more than clothes. But seek his kingdom, and these things will be given to you as well" (Luke 12:29-31).

Everything you own belongs to God, and He made it possible for you to have it by providing the money. Nothing you own on earth can be taken to heaven. Job tells us "Naked I came from my mother's womb, and naked I will depart. The Lord gave and the Lord has taken away; may the name of the Lord be praised" (Job 1:21).

Being jealous about the things others own keeps you from appreciating the many blessings God has given you. It takes your mind off God's priorities and interests. Paul tells us in Romans 13:13, "Let us behave decently . . . not in dissension and jealousy," and in Galatians, "The acts of the sinful nature are obvious: . . . hatred, discord, jealousy" (5:19-20).

The next time you envy a friend who has something you wish you had, think of your blessings and thank God for them. When you hear someone bragging about the bigger, more expensive things they have or plan to buy, remember that "things" aren't what matters to God, but instead, the attitude of the heart.

Additional Verses

1. "You shall not covet your neighbor's wife. You shall not set your desire on your neighbor's house or land, his manservant or maidservant, his ox or donkey, or anything that belongs to your neighbor" (Deut. 5:21).

2. "A heart at peace gives life to the body, but envy rots the bones" (Prov. 14:30).

3. "Let us not become conceited, provoking and envying each other" (Gal. 5:26).

4. "But if you harbor bitter envy and selfish ambition in your hearts, do not boast about it or deny the truth. For where you have envy and selfish ambition, there you find disorder and every evil practice" (Jas. 3:14,16).

Implications for the Older Child

Kevin Huggins points out that adult expectations of teens can be overwhelming and stressful. In an attempt to reach these expectations, teens try to emulate the model found in TV and the movies. As a result, they look at their own bodies and find them inferior. Huggins adds, ". . . kids compensate any way they can—often devoting obsessive attention to such things as clothing, hair styles, dieting, body building and cosmetics."[3]

Thus, a teenager who appears to be jealous of a more attractively dressed friend may simply be reflecting a desire not to "stand out in a crowd," not to appear different from the others in his group. By dressing differently or not wearing the latest "in" brand, he fears he will come across to contemporaries as an "odd ball."

How can you help a child develop the ability to handle this situation? While a teen may reject "Why do you want to be like everyone else?" or "We can't afford it," he may accept logical reasoning. By arming him with logical arguments against the purchase of a particular brand of shoes (poor quality), for example, he can face opponents, ready to battle for his right to choose.

There are some teenagers, however, who are unable to make these value judgments at this time in life. In this case, a parent might work to substitute an acceptable alternative. If finances are a concern, the mother or the daughter might think about sewing a dress, copying a favored style. If finances are not involved, it might be well to evaluate your own objections. Ask yourself if this is a major issue with future implications or a relatively insignificant concern. Will it affect your child's final well-being?

Remember that most of these decisions are insignificant when related to the development of a strong character. Don't deprive your child of acceptance by peers simply because of one of your own prejudices or biases.

Make certain you can show your child specific biblical causes for your decision. Sit down with your teen and read the Bible verse together, allowing time for open discussion. The child will respect you for holding biblical convictions but he may lose respect if you are merely repeating social and cultural biases.

24
My Parents Make Me Go to Church Every Sunday. Why Is Going to Church So Important?

When we become Christians, we become part of a big family—God's family. God wants us to meet together and work together as part of His family. Then we represent Jesus to our world. God even calls us Jesus' body. "Just as each of us has one body with many parts, . . . so in Christ we who are many form one body, and each member belongs to all others" (Rom. 12:45). Paul wrote that each member of the church is needed by the others. This makes the church complete.

To learn how to be Jesus' representative in the world, you need to meet with others to study God's Word. You can encourage each other to grow closer to Him. The meeting is a time to worship God and thank Him for all He has done. If He is the center of your life, you will want to be with others who love Him, too.

Listen to the author of Hebrews.

> And let us consider how we may spur one another on toward love and good deeds. Let us not give up meeting together, as some are in the habit of doing, but let us encourage one another (10:24-25).

God wants us to go to church, setting aside a time that is just for Him. There we worship Him and learn with others how to love Him more.

Additional Verses

1. "The body is a unit, though it is made up of many parts; and though all its parts are many, they form one body. So it is with Christ" (1 Cor. 12:12).

2. "After all, no one ever hated his own body, but he

feeds and cares for it, just as Christ does the church—for we are members of his body" (Eph. 5:29).

3. "Now you are the body of Christ, and each one of you is a part of it" (1 Cor. 12:27).

4. "They devoted themselves to the apostles' teaching and to the fellowship, to the breaking of bread and to prayer. Every day they continued to meet together in the temple courts" (Acts 2:42).

Further Insights

Arthur Murray writes,

Christ's commission to His Church through Peter shows the place the little ones have in His heart and teaches us to think of the weakness, the value, the need, and the hope of our children. . . . The Church of the next generation, the servants with whom, in but a few years' time, Jesus will do His work of converting and saving and blessing men, are the children of today.[4]

Dick Day notes,

One of the primary means God used to propagate the church of Jesus Christ was relationships. . . . It's interesting to note that the fastest growing churches today are rooted in the sociological principle of support groups, of family systems.[5]

Judith Allen Shelly says,

When children are constantly nourished in the faith through prayer and Bible teaching in the context of a loving family and supportive Christian community, they are likely to encounter the living God and develop a deep and stable faith."[6]

Implications for the Older Child

Many teenagers refuse to attend church because they find the Sunday School and youth program boring, outdated, not geared to the interests and problems of the young. Many churches fail to see the importance of a well-trained, dedicated youth minister. Thus, the same old teaching methods are handed down from disgruntled adult to disgruntled adult, stressed by the inattention and even insolence of the children they try to teach.

Parents can help by describing the value of church attendance in their own young lives, citing specific incidents and results. In addition, they can encourage their church leaders to install a relevant youth ministry in the church.

Ken Crosswhite, a pastor in Atlanta, Georgia, with eleven years of youth work experience says,

> People minimize the spiritual warfare that goes on in young people, and they have not grasped the fact that youth are the most spiritually responsive people in our society. During adolescence they make some of the major decisions of life—choosing a master, a mate and a mission.[7]

By encouraging your teen to become an active participant in the youth program of the church and also encouraging your church to improve these programs, family and church can work together to guide a child to a successful God-led life.

Remember that Christ designed and authorized the church and said, "Where two or three have gathered together in my name, there I am in their midst" (Matt. 18:20, NASB). Explain to your child that we go to church to meet the living Lord. Is there any better reason for being there?

25

When I Earn Money, Daddy Says I Should Give Some of It to Jesus. Why Does God Want My Money? What Does It Mean to Tithe?

Tina jerked her blue-stained fingers away from the thorny blackberry bush. She stared at the bloody scratch on her arm. *Boy, is it hot!* she thought. A salty drop of perspiration dripped from her brunette bangs into her eyes. She rubbed her stinging eyes and sat down on a dirt pile to rest. Looking at the fruit of her labor, she grinned. *Job well done*, she thought.

Tina turned the bucket from side to side and picked out unripe red berries from the juicy black ones. *So beautiful. The best of the season.* The sun's rays burned her scratched arm as she sniffed the fragrance of the neighbor's newly mown grass.

Time to get up and earn some money. She picked up the bucket and headed toward the nearest street. Going from door to door, she smiled at the pleased neighbors who dropped shiny quarters and dimes into her outstretched hand in exchange for pints of her carefully selected berries. As she walked, she enjoyed the sound of the coins clinking in the pocket of her shorts.

When she arrived home, her dad smiled at the bulging pockets. "Looks like you've been well-paid for a hard day's work, Tina," he said.

Tina grinned. "It's the most I've ever earned."

"What are you going to do with all that money, Dear? I hope you'll give some to God to thank Him for a profitable day."

Tina's face clouded. "I was going to save if for that shiny blue bike we saw at Jones Hardware Store, Dad. Why does God want the money anyway?"

Adult Response

God allows us to earn money for the things we need and want. We must not forget that the money is God's. He lends it to us and expects us to be good stewards of it. That means He wants us to use it wisely.

Trouble comes when we forget that the money belongs to God first—His gift to us. We start spending it without praying about it and then buy things we don't need. We don't make good use of God's money. Before we even realize it, we forget that God gave us the money. We begin to spend it unwisely and then may think that the money is ours alone. We may even start to love money more than we love God.

Jesus warned us many times about this misplaced love. "No one can serve two masters. Either he will hate the one and love the other, or he will be devoted to the one and despise the other. You cannot serve both God and Money" (Matt.6:24).

Throughout the Bible, there are many other warnings about money and how we use it. Wanting to protect us from loving money more than we love Him and knowing that this love would cause us much sadness and pain, God decided we should first return part of it to Him before spending any. Then we would remember that it belongs to Him and He gave it to us.

In the Old Testament God began a method that we follow today. He told His nation, Israel, "A tithe of everything from the land, whether grain from the soil or fruit from the trees, belongs to the Lord; it is holy to the Lord" (Lev. 27:30). A tithe is a tenth of all we earn. Paul told the Corinthians to do a similar thing with their giving.

Paul said, "On the first day of every week, each one of you should set aside a sum of money in keeping with his income, saving it up, so that when I come, no collections will have to be made" (1 Cor. 16:2).

When God provides you with money, thank Him and show Him your gratitude by returning a tenth to Him. Give it to the work of Christ's kingdom. Be careful always that you don't begin to love money and the things it buys more than you love God (1 Cor. 16:2).

Additional Verses

1. "Whoever loves money never has money enough; whoever loves wealth is never satisfied with his income. This too is meaningless" (Eccl. 5:10).

2. "But godliness with contentment is great gain. For we brought nothing into the world, and we can take nothing out of it. But if we have food and clothing, we will be content with that. People who want to get rich fall into temptation and a trap and into many foolish and harmful desires that plunge men into ruin and destruction. For the love of money is a root of all kinds of evil" (1 Tim. 6:6-10).

3. "Keep your lives free from the love of money and be content with what you have, because God has said, 'Never will I leave you; never will I forsake you' " (Heb. 13:5).

Further Insights

Rod and Judy Blue say, "Many parents go through a process of 'training' their children to manage money without having any idea about what they want to teach or what their training objectives are."[8]

They add that the four principles are: (1) God owns it all; (2) there is a trade-off between time-and-effort and money-rewards; (3) there is no such thing as an "independent" financial decision; and (4) delayed gratification is the key to financial maturity.

The four skills include developing a one-year spending plan, buying wisely, making decisions, and setting goals.

Implications for the Older Child

Many decisions your teen makes about money are based on peer choices. Wearing name-brand shoes, designer jeans, or a particular hairstyle may be pleas for acceptance. Even when you reject such choices affecting the way money is spent, you should face the fact that it matters to your child. How can you help your child develop the ability to break away from the influence of peers?

Open communication is the first choice. Discuss peer pressure with your teen—its positive and negative effects. Point out that the way we spend our money should be based on Christian values. Discuss the negative aspects of doing and acting like all others. Assure your child that God sees each of us as an individual with unique qualities.

After talking about peer influence on spending choices, go to the Bible for answers. It is said the use of money is mentioned around seven hundred times there. Ecclesiastes 5:10—"He who loves money will not be satisfied with money"(NASB).

In Matthew 21:12-13 we read,

> And Jesus entered the temple and cast out all those who were buying and selling in the temple . . . and He said to them, "It is written, 'My house shall be called a House of Prayer,' but you are making it a robber's den."

1 Timothy 6:10 says, "For the love of money is a root of all sorts of evil, and some by longing for it have wandered away from the faith" (NASB).

Encourage your teen to develop a plan for the use of money, setting aside the tithe and savings first before making other purchases. Strengthen his ability to say "no" to the demands of peers by being open to questions, reinforcing good qualities, and maintaining communication during these difficult growing years.

The psalmist tells us, "The law of thy mouth is better to

me than thousands of gold and silver pieces" (Ps. 119:72, NASB). We fool ourselves if we think we would be better off if we had more money. It's simply not true. Some of the happiest people are poor financially but rich in the knowledge of God's love and Word, in faith, and in the love of their friends and family.

Section IV
How Can I Live a Life that Pleases God?
Questions About Faith

Section IV
How Can I Live a Life that Pleases God?
Questions About Faith

A young child mentally stores a wealth of concrete information received from Sunday School, church programs, and family devotions and instruction. Incorporated with that knowledge is a multitude of impressions collected from interactions with people who communicate this material that is also stored in the child's memory. Included are memories of treatment by church leaders and family members.

As the child matures, he or she begins searching for ways to apply the biblical knowledge that has been received. She desires to "flesh out" the biblical truth and relate it to her daily life. This desire challenges the emerging teenager to plunge deeper into the implications of her beliefs.

The "how to's" become the issue. The thoughts: *How can I get to know God better? show Him I love Him? know my prayers are answers?* surface. At this time, encouraging your child to apply his or her beliefs does a lot to build faith.

Concerning this, I am reminded of a time when my oldest daughter, age eleven, asked me to pray for her. "God always seems to answer your prayers," she said. "I don't think He hears mine." Immediately I knew she was expressing the deeper question of God's involvement in her personal life.

I remembered something I had done at a similar time

in my life. To assure myself of God's response to my prayers, I began to list and record answers. This tangible expression of spiritual reality did much to build my young faith. I watched as God answered prayer after prayer, working out a host of concerns and situations. Something I knew intellectually—that God heard and answered prayers—became personal. God heard and answered *my* prayers.

As you help your child grow in faith, encourage her active participation in personal Christian growth by keeping a daily journal, by listing prayer requests, and by underlining Bible verses related to an area of concern. Encourage her to set aside a time for daily devotions and Bible study, using inductive materials requiring written answers to the questions. This helps her to make personal practical application of Bible truth. Think of enrolling her in Christian youth meetings and summer camps.

Probably one of the most helpful methods of helping your child see biblical truth "lived out" is through your own daily life. By seeing you involved in daily Bible study, your child will have a better understanding of a life of faith and help her learn how to live the Bible-based Christian life that pleases God.

26
Where Can I Find Out More About God?

Adult Response

God doesn't want to be a stranger to you. Since you are unable to see God and talk with Him the same way you would another person, how can you find out what He is like? Even though you cannot see Him or touch Him, He is real. There are three ways you can find out about God: through the things He made, His creation; through His words, the Bible; and Jesus, His Son.

You can learn about God by looking at the things He made. We read, "For since the *creation* of the world, God's invisible qualities [attributes] . . . have been clearly seen, being understood from what has been made" (Rom. 1:20).

When we see the greatness of the mountains and seas, the beauty of the sunrise and sunset, the many colored flowers, the changing seasons, we realize God has many sides to His character. His character ways are called His attributes, and you can learn more about these through viewing His creation.

You also learn about these ways through His words found in the *Bible*. Long ago, God chose certain men to record everything He wants you to know about Himself in the Bible. It is God's personal message to you. You learn that God's attributes are special because they never change. God always remains the same. The things you learn about God in the Bible today will be true about God for the rest of your life.

The only way you can *know* God is by learning about *His Son, Jesus Christ*. Through creation and the Bible you can learn about God but only by believing in Jesus Christ can you know God personally. God sent Jesus to all the world so that all people, including you and I, will have a greater understanding of what our Heavenly Father is like. But belief in Jesus alone allows us to know who He is. ("No one comes to the Father but by me," John 14:6.)

In Hebrews 1:1-4, we read,

> God . . . in these last days has spoken to us by his Son, whom he appointed heir of all things, and through whom he made the universe. The Son is the radiance of God's glory and the exact representation of his being, sustaining all things by his powerful word.

Additional Verses

1. "The heavens declare the glory of God; the skies proclaim the work of his hands. Day after day they pour forth speech; night after night they display knowledge. There is no speech or language where their voice is not heard. Their voice goes out into all the earth, their words to the ends of the world" (Ps. 19:1-4).

2. "For everything that was written in the past was written to teach us, so that through endurance and the encouragement of the Scriptures we might have hope" (Rom. 15:4).

3. "All Scripture is God-breathed and is useful for teaching, rebuking, correcting and training in righteousness" (2 Tim. 3:16).

4. "For he has . . . brought us into the kingdom of the Son he loves, in whom we have redemption, the forgiveness of sins. He is the image of the invisible God, the firstborn over all creation. For by him all things were created; things in heaven and on earth, visible and invisible. . . . He is before all things, and in him all things hold together. And he is the head of the body, the church; he is the beginning and the firstborn from among the dead, so that in everything he might have supremacy. For God was

pleased to have all his fullness dwell in him, and through him to reconcile to himself all things, whether things on earth or things in heaven, by making peace through his blood, shed on the cross" (Col. 1:13-20).

Further Insights

Paul Lewis writes,

What will it take to give your child a mature and passionate love for God? What are you modeling on the stage of family life? Timothy's sincere faith first dwelt in his grandmother, Lois, and his mother, Eunice (2 Tim. 1:5). Your children won't catch something you don't have. In fact, if your spiritual life is weak it will only immunize them from catching the real thing.[1]

Implications for the Older Child

We should encourage a teen to turn to the Bible, God's inspired Word, to learn more about God. A searching look at Jesus' life can be a source of satisfaction to both child and parent. By following Jesus through His ministry, His work, His actions, and reactions, parents can help their child learn of God as seen in His Son. A study of the Old Testament teaches of God's covenant agreement and love for His people Israel. All of history is "His story" and reveals the Person of our God.

Yet, your teen who is in a questioning period may want to seek information from other sources. It's important to keep an open mind about questions and to be prepared to provide guidance in the search for answers. Don't brush off the hard questions. Examine all available evidence.

First look at archeological finds. Paul E. Little, in *Know Why You Believe*, quotes Miller Burrows of Yale as saying that archeology supports the reliability of the scriptural record. Archeology should not be used as proof however that the Bible is correct. Only the Holy Spirit working in the heart of a person can do that. However, archeology gives us a clearer understanding of the biblical record and message. We are able to see the Old Testament background in the over 25,000 sites studied in the Middle East. Sir Frederic Kenyon, a noted archeologist with the British Victorian Institute, said, "To my mind, the true and valuable thing to say about archeology is not that it proves the Bible but that it illustrates the Bible."[2]

Other proof of the historical accuracy of the Bible can be found in the writings of Josephus, a first-century Jewish historian. Josh McDowell's books *More Than a Carpenter* and *Evidence that Demands a Verdict* as well as Frank Morrison's *Who Moved the Stone?* challenge the teen to examine the evidence for biblical truth.

At times you can reinforce your teen's understanding about God through his own experiences. By describing God's specific responses to your prayers made in faith as well as those made by others, you can help your child see that the Holy Spirit of God is working in the Christian's life even when he is unaware of it. Explain that by trusting Him and asking forgiveness for sins, He will reveal Himself through answered prayer and manifest Himself through life's daily endeavors. (John 14:21).

27
What Does It Mean to Love God?

The first way we can show God we love Him is to believe in His Son. God spoke from a cloud about Jesus in Mark 9:7, "This is my Son, whom I love. Listen to him!" Later, Jesus said, "No one comes to the Father except through me" (John 14:6).

God sent His son, Jesus Christ, to pay the penalty for our sins so our relationship with Him could be restored.

Sometimes it's hard to understand that we are all sinners, but it's true. Not one person except Jesus has ever lived a perfect life or done everything to please God. We all do things we regret or are ashamed of. Because of this, God sent Jesus to show us how to live and to take away our sins through His death and resurrection.

God can't look upon sin; so since we've all sinned, we couldn't become His friends. Through believing in Jesus Christ, who died to take away our sins, we can know that God considers us His child. To say we love God is to say we love and believe in His Son.

Also, we show God our love by obeying His Word and His Son. Jesus tells us, "Whoever has my commands and obeys them, he is the one who loves me. He who loves me will be loved by my Father, I too will love him and show myself to him" (John 14:21).

He also said, "If anyone loves me, he will obey my teaching. My Father will love him, and we will come to him and make our home with him. He who does not love me will not obey my teaching. These words you hear are not my own, they belong to the Father who sent me" (vv. 23-24).

Another way you show God your love is to obey your parents. "Children, obey your parents in everything, for this pleases the Lord" (Col. 3:20).

We show God we love Him by telling Him we are glad we belong to Him and by asking Him to help us become the person He created us to be for His glory. Then we can experience His plans and purposes for our life. He promises us when we do this that, ". . . in all things God works for the good of those who love him, who have been called according to his purpose" (Rom. 8:28).

Additional Verses

1. "Therefore, I urge you, brothers, in view of God's mercy, to offer your bodies as living sacrifices, holy and

pleasing God—this is your spiritual act of worship. Do not conform any longer to the pattern of this world, but be transformed by the renewing of your mind. Then you will be able to test and approve what God's will is—his good, pleasing and perfect will" (Rom. 12:1-2).

2. "He has showed you, O man, what is good. And what does the Lord require of you? To act justly and to love mercy and to walk humbly with your God" (Mic. 6:8).

Further Insights

Judith Allen Shelly writes,

> The need for love and relatedness is basic to survival. As the growing child becomes secure in the love of parents and other caring adults, he or she begins to love others and understand God's love.[3]

Paul Lewis says,

> In Proverbs 22:6, God promises you can give your child a heart for him. It's an ongoing process of mutual growth each day that will have immediate joys—and eternal rewards.[4]

Implications for the Older Child

Children have learned from their youngest days that God is love and that God loves each of His children. But many don't understand that the love *of* God demands love *for* God. Teens, egocentric and introspective, may not know how to love God or see the need for it.

It is said that to love someone, you must know that person thoroughly. If this is true then the way for a teen to love God is to know God, to know all about Him.

In February 1987, *Worldwide Challenge* magazine reported on a survey they made of high-school students. Asked how parents could help them spiritually, they learned that teens want:

(1) parents to talk to them about God and their faith.

(2) to have more open discussions of religion, God, and God's love.

(3) their parents to pray for them.

To talk about loving God, stress the attributes of God and focus on the love God has for His children. Help the child to see that God's personal love and concern for us demand a response of love and thanksgiving from us. By appreciating and obeying God's Word, offering praises and thanksgiving to God for who He is, and by exemplifying God's love to others, we are expressing our love to God.

Paul, writing to the Ephesians, told them, "Therefore be imitators of God, as beloved children and walk in love just as Christ also loved you" (Eph. 5:1-2, NASB). The best way to respond lovingly to God is to follow Jesus' example.

Remind your children of Christ's new commandment that we love each other as He loved us (John 13:34-35). Explain that when we accept Jesus Christ as our Savior, the Holy Spirit dwells in us. The Bible tells us that the fruit of the Spirit is love, joy, peace, patience, kindness, goodness, faithfulness, generosity, self-control (Gal. 5:22-23); all attributes of God Himself.

28

When I Do Something Wrong, I Feel Guilty. What Is God's Forgiveness and How Do I Know He Forgives When I Ask?

Karen's blouse clung to her skin from the summer heat. Perspiration dripped from her freckled forehead. *School in August is miserable*, she thought. *Why do we have to start so early?*

Karen trudged the few blocks from school to her home. The screen door slammed behind her as she entered the sunny yellow kitchen. The odor of her leftover sandwich caused her nose to wrinkle as she dropped the remains in the garbage can.

Her mom and dad were at work. Bored at the thought of being in the house without anything to do, she murmured "What now?" then decided to walk downtown to the drugstore for a coke and candy bar. *Why not?* she reasoned. She knew her parents didn't want her to leave the house after school, but they'd never know. They weren't here.

"Why shouldn't I go to the store? Why is it wrong if no one else knows?" she said aloud.

A picture of Mr. Johnson's face flashed through her mind. She remembered her Sunday School teacher's voice, "Have you ever felt guilty for something you did wrong even though no one else knew about it?" Karen decided to go to the drugstore after all. Her mind trailed off as she thought of the questions Mr. Johnson had written on the blackboard.

When I do something wrong, why do I feel so guilty?
What is God's forgiveness?
How do I know He forgives when I ask?

Adult Response

God gives us very specific guidelines for life in the Bible. He knows what's best for us because He created us. Following these guidelines are the only way to really experience and enjoy the life God has planned for us. That's why when we do something wrong, our conscience tells us.

David experienced this. We read, "Afterward, David was conscience-stricken for having cut off a corner of his [Saul's] robe" (1 Sam. 24:5). God gave us a conscience so we would feel guilty when we disobey God's Words. He wants us to turn to Him to find forgiveness.

We receive God's forgiveness when we believe on His Son's death as the payment for our sin and sin's removal. Sin is that thing within us that makes us want to do the wrong thing—to disobey God. When we believe in Jesus Christ, He gives us a clear conscience. We read in Hebrews 9:4 that because Jesus died for us, "How much more, then, will the blood of Christ, who through the eternal Spirit offered himself unblemished to God, cleanse our consciences from acts that lead to death, so that we may serve the living God!."

Paul told Timothy the importance of a good and clean conscience, "Timothy, my son, I give you this instruction, ... so that by following them you may fight the good fight, by holding on to faith and a good conscience. Some have rejected these and so have shipwrecked their faith" (1 Tim. 1:18-19). This was so important to Paul he could say, "My brothers, I have fulfilled my duty to God in all good conscience to this day" (Acts 23:1). And "So I strive always to keep my conscience clear before God and man" (Acts 24:16).

Additional Verses

1. "Now this is our boast: Our conscience testifies that we have conducted ourselves in the world, and especially in our relations with you, in the holiness and sincerity that are from God" (2 Cor. 1:12).

2. "Therefore, brothers, since we have confidence to enter the Most Holy Place by the blood of Jesus, by a new and living way opened for us through the curtain, that is, his body, and since we have a great priest over the house of God, let us draw near to God with a sincere heart in full assurance of faith, having our hearts sprinkled to cleanse us from a guilty conscience and having our bodies washed with pure water" (Heb. 10:19-22).

3. ". . . and this water symbolized baptism that now saves you also—not the removal of dirt from the body but the pledge of a good conscience toward God" (1 Pet. 3:21).

Further Insights

"The earliest awareness of moral conscience is simple," Ted Ward says in *Values Begin at Home*.

> Some things are right and some things are wrong. The child's moral sense is thus developed. It is important that the child's relationship with the major source of those clues, the parents, be filled with respect and love.[5]

Implications for the Older Child

Teens are in the process of changing from receiving, accepting learners to a questioning, doubting ones. They are developing the ability to think abstractly and to project their thoughts into the future. Christian parents should welcome conversations with their teens to explore their thoughts about God, His laws, and relationships with His children.

When your teen asks you about believing, forgiveness, and guilt, beware of giving pat answers or stifling discussions that result from honest, open searching. Follow these steps: (1) *Listen* to the questions and concerns carefully. (2) *Pray* with him/her that God will reveal His answers. (3) *Search* the Scriptures together for His Word. (4) *Look* at the lives of others for direction that point the way to the results of both right and wrong decisions.

There are many references in the Bible to help you and your teen come to a satisfactory conclusion. Numbers 14:11-12 tells of God's words to Moses about the nonbelieving Israelites. Look at Psalm 78:21-22 as well as Matthew 21:22 and Mark 9:23. In the Book of Acts we find,

Therefore, my brothers, I want you to know that through Jesus the forgiveness of sins is proclaimed to you. Through him everyone who believes is justified from everything you could not be justified from by the law of Moses (13:38-39).

This promise includes freedom from guilt when sins are sincerely confessed.

29
Why Is It Important for Me to Pray? Does God Really Hear My Prayers?

Adult Response

Prayer is important because that is how we talk with God. Through prayer, we get to know Him better and learn what His plans are for us. God promises in His Bible that when we pray, He hears us. David wrote, "O you who hear prayer, to you all men will come" (Ps.65:2) and "Praise be to God who has not rejected my prayer or withheld his love from me!" (Ps. 66:20).

God promises that He hears our prayers and answers. The answer may be "yes," "no," or "wait," but He does answer when we pray in Jesus' name. Jesus tells us in Matthew 21:22, "If you believe, you will receive whatever you ask for in prayer."

Prayer is answered according to God's best and perfect will for us. Even when our feelings may tell us God isn't listening or won't answer, we can remember that our feelings aren't dependable; but God's Word is. God always keeps His word.

If you are having a difficult time believing that God hears and answers your prayers, begin a project today. In a notebook, list your prayer requests each day. Put a column for the day's date, your request, and another column for God's answer.

Each time God answers your prayer, note it beside the request. You'll be excited to see how God is actively answering your prayers. Your faith in God and His desire to hear and answer your prayers will grow stronger each day.

Additional Verses

1. "And when you pray, do not be like the hypocrites, for they love to pray standing in the synagogues and on the street corners to be seen by men. I tell you the truth, they have received their reward in full. But when you pray, go into your room, close the door and pray to your Father, who is unseen. Then your Father who sees what is done in secret, will reward you. And when you pray, do not keep on babbling like pagans, for they think they will be heard because of their many words. Do not be like them, for your Father knows what you need before you ask him" (Matt. 6:5-8)

2. "Therefore confess your sins to each other and pray for each other so that you may be healed. The prayer of a righteous man is powerful and effective." (Jas. 5:16)

3. "For the eyes of the Lord are on the righteous and his ears are attentive to their prayer." (1 Pet. 3:12).

Further Insights

E. V. Hill writes,

> There is power in prayer. Much prayer, much power. No prayer, no power. . . .
>
> PRAYER is a live option. It is not just a number on the program. It is not just being courteous to God, respectful to God. It is the appointed way God has permitted us worm-like creatures to approach Him in Jesus' name. Learn to pray.[6]

Implications for the Older Child

Some people pray only when they feel out of control of situations in their lives. They go to God as a last resort, thinking that their desires will be met and problems solved. This is not necessarily the end result. Then we hear the cry, "Where was God when I needed Him?"

To help your teen understand the rich benefits of a life of prayer beyond the expected "yes," talk about the purpose of prayer. Through prayer, we communicate with God; we learn who He is, what He expects of us, His children, and receive His guidance as we strive to do His will.

Explain the necessity of developing a commitment to pray. Encourage your teen to develop a plan for a prayer life. One teenage boy sets his alarm an hour early in the morning to have time to seek God's will.

When your child complains that God isn't hearing her and that her prayers are being ignored, discuss the methods by which God answers prayers.

Many of us think that an automatic "yes" is the one and only answer when we pray. We decide what we want and then direct God to come through. However, God's answer may not be the expected one. At times He will say "yes" if it's in His will because He loves us and wants the best for us.

At other times, a wait may be required. He may use this method to test our faith and encourage us to endure the trials that hinder us (Jas. 1:2-4). Since we know God wants the best for His children, we can be certain He is doing what is best in each particular incident (Ps. 27:13-14).

Then there are the times when "no" is the answer. A "no" is a difficult decision for young people to accept, especially if he or she thinks all answers from God are "yes." Remind your teen of the times "no" was the correct response in your own life. Talk about Joni Eareckson, paralyzed in a diving accident, who prayed for healing. Instead God uses her to reach out to both handicapped and able people as an example of His faithfulness and joy in adversity. Check out of the library or buy one of her books for your teen to read.

Some of the reasons God says no include (1) when there is unconfessed sin in our lives (Ps. 66:18); (2) when our motives are wrong (Jas. 4:3); or (3) when He can use us and our problems for His purposes. Even the apostle Paul's prayer was refused by God (2 Cor. 12:7-9). Remind your teen that God uses refusals to encourage us to depend on Him, to trust Him, and to experience His power in our weakness.

Other Scriptures to consult: Isaiah 59:1-2, James 5:17, John 11:1-6,17,38-45.

30
What Does It Mean to *Trust* God?

Sandra entered the lunchroom, thirsty and hungry. P.E. that morning had been rough. She was exhausted after running around the football field six times training for athletic tests.

She reached into her pocketbook. "Oh, no," she groaned. "I forgot my lunch money. Of all times, it would have to happen on a day when I'm so hungry," she grumbled.

Putting her purse on the cafeteria table, she moved past the tables, crowded with children, eating and talking. Then she saw it. Not two feet away lay a dollar bill, a quarter, and a dime. Just enough for lunch.

She looked around to see if it belonged to anyone. No one was around. Quickly glancing from side to side, she grabbed the money and stuffed it in her pocket. As she walked away she thought, *Someone must have dropped it by accident. Obviously they didn't need it*, she rationalized.

She purchased her lunch and joined other children, still busy talking.

"Hey," Matthew shouted, "Where's my lunch money? Somebody stole my money!"

Sandra felt her face heat up as she glanced around the room. No one looked at her. She was safe. She hadn't been seen. Bending her head over her plate, she continued to eat.

Her theft undiscovered, Sandra left the lunchroom. Although she was relieved, she felt guilty. As the day went on, she became more and more troubled. She waited anxiously for her dad to pick her up early for her dental appointment.

Settled in the car seat beside him, she suddenly burst into tears.

Puzzled, her father said, "What is it, Sandra, Honey?" Gulping back her tears, she poured out her story.

Her dad paused, then said, "Sandra, you know what you did today was wrong. Stealing is absolutely wrong, no matter how great your need seemed to be."

"I know, Dad," Sandra agreed. She felt miserable, knowing what she had done was wrong. "But, Dad, what can I do about it now? If anybody finds out, they'll never speak to me again."

"Sandra, you know what you have to do. You must return the money to the boy. Then, trust God to handle the situation for you. God will honor your desire to admit you're wrong and make it right with Him."

"How can I trust God? Will God help me even though I did something wrong?"

"God is able. He will help you when you admit you are wrong and try to make amends," her father said, patting her shoulder.

Adult Response

When you sit in a chair at school, do you stop to examine it each time to be sure it is sturdy and will hold you? No, you simply sit down and trust that it will not crumple. Trust in God is like that. We act on the fact that we believe in Him and completely trust Him to answer our prayers about everything that concerns us.

Trusting God is believing that He is able to help you in your time of need. God loves you. He wants the best for you and He is in control of all life. God is in charge of everything. Paul tells us about Jesus Christ,

> For by him all things were created: things in heaven and on earth, visible and invisible, whether thrones or powers or rulers or authorities; all things were created by him and for him. He is before all things, and in him all things hold together (Col. 1:16-17).

Later in the book, we discuss the fact that God is sovereign, knows everything, and has the power to act on our behalf. (See questions, 33, 38, and 39.) Your trust is more than a matter of knowing these things with your mind. It means acting upon them as true and believing them with your heart.

In a situation where you know you are wrong, you must attempt to make it right. God knows the incident. He knows what you have done, how others will react to your actions. He knows everything about the situation. Now you must trust Him to work it all out as you obey Him and follow His instructions found in the Bible.

We must exercise our faith and trust that God will honor our obedience to His Word. The author of Hebrews writes, "And without faith it is impossible to please God, because anyone who comes to him must believe that he exists and that he rewards those who earnestly seek him"

(11:6). Even when things we plan do not work out immediately, we can rely on Him because He knows the bigger picture as He works things out according to His will.

Trust is relying on God without a back-up plan. It is knowing that He never fails and He will do what is right and best for you. Realizing that you can depend on Him completely, you trust Him in everything you do and in every situation.

Additional Verses

1. "Those who know your name will trust in you, for you, Lord, have never forsaken those who seek you" (Ps. 9:10).

2. "In you our fathers put their trust; they trusted and you delivered them. They cried to you and were saved; in you they trusted and were not disappointed" (Ps. 22:4-5).

3. "Trust in the Lord with all your heart and lean not on your own understanding; in all your ways acknowledge him, and he will make your paths straight" (Prov. 3:5-6).

4. "Cast all your anxiety on him because he cares for you" (1 Pet. 5:7).

Further Insights

Michael W. Smith says in *Old Enough to Know,*

> Jesus Christ is the ultimate Friend. He is the Light that holds you in the darkness—the Candle burning in the wind. Through Him you lean upon the Father and find the strength you need for this life[7]

Raymond and Dorothy Moore write,

> . . . a baby must first learn to trust someone to love and care for him. Preferably this is his parents. . . .
>
> The sense of trust thus established determines the basis of trust in a higher being, his God.[8]

Implications for the Older Child

From the beginning of life, young children trust their parents to provide love, food, and shelter. There is no written contract or book stating that this trust is justified or warranted. It is blind. As they grow older, they lose that childlike trust and seek independence.

Christians have the Bible to point the way in their search for faith and trust in the Lord (Ps.4:5). There, we learn that faith and trust go hand-in-hand. David, a shepherd, compared himself to his sheep in their complete dependence; they on him and he on the Lord. He trusted that God, His shepherd, would lead him safely through life—if he put his life in God's hands.

Billy Graham, in his April 11, 1991, newspaper column wrote, "True faith is not just believing certain facts about God, true faith means that we commit our lives to Christ in trust and obedience, believing and trusting His promises of salvation."[9]

To trust means to submit, to be humble, and to be willing to accept God's plan for life. We are told that by trusting Him we will be established (successful) (2 Chron. 20:20), have an everlasting Rock upon which to depend (Isa. 26:4), and have eternal life (2 Cor. 1:9).

Encourage your teen to develop a lasting belief and trust in God as she seeks His will. Help her to understand that Christians aren't assured a trouble-free life. Yet by trusting God, she can feel assured that God will be with her through adversity and pain, working all things for her best (Rom. 8:28). God will provide the inner strength she needs to deal with problems when she trusts Him and seeks His will.

31
Does God Have a Plan for My Life?
Is There a Reason I Am Alive?

Adult Response

Why are you alive? God wants you to know Him and love Him. He chose you to become His child before the world was formed. First you must accept His Son, Jesus and believe in Him. Paul wrote to the Romans, "For those God foreknew he also predestined to be conformed to the likeness of his Son, that he might be the firstborn among many brothers" (Rom. 8:29). This means God wants you to be like Jesus so that others will come to know God.

God's rich love caused Him to send Jesus so our sins could be forgiven and we could have a relationship with God through Him. "For he chose us in him before the creation of the world to be holy and blameless in his sight. In love he predestined us to be adopted as his sons through Jesus Christ, in accordance with his pleasure and will" (Eph. 1:4-6). We are alive to become God's child through faith in Jesus Christ and to tell others about Him.

God knows you completely, everything you are and do, and He watches over you with love and caring. David tells us in Psalm 139, "O Lord, you have searched me and you know me. You know when I sit and when I rise; you perceive my thoughts from afar. You discern my going out and my lying down; you are familiar with all my ways. Before a word is on my tongue you know it completely, O Lord" (vv. 1-5). God has a plan for your life—a plan which He knows is best for you. Paul explains that before you were born, God planned certain things you are to accomplish in your life (Eph. 2:10).

God told Jeremiah, " 'For I know the plans I have for you,' declares the Lord, 'plans to prosper you and not to harm you, plans to give you hope and a future. You will seek me and find me when you seek me with all your heart' " (Jer. 29:11,13). All of us are alive to know God and to know the joy of fulfilling His plans for us. There is no greater purpose or challenge than this.

Additional Verses

1. "The Lord Almighty has sworn, 'Surely, as I have planned, so it will be, and as I have purposed, so it will stand.' For the Lord Almighty has purposed and who can thwart him? His hand is stretched out, and who can turn it back?" (Isa. 14:24,27)

2. "I know that you can do all things, no plan of yours can be thwarted" (Job 42:2).

3. "In his heart a man plans his course, but the Lord determines his steps" (Prov. 16:9).

Implications for the Older Child

Independent teens may be bothered by the idea that God controls their lives and guides decision making. We realize that because God loves us, He also wants us to love Him and to live for Him. He offers help so we will make the right decisions when we acknowledge He is our Lord. Philip Yancey, writing for "Radio Bible Class," says that we receive "quiet nudges" from God to help us make choices. As we study God's Word, He gives us direction and guidance.

Parents, looking back on their lives, can identify the times they recognized these nudges. Some who look backward can highlight a period of indecision about a choice that proved in time to be decided by God's intervention in circumstances or events (Ps. 32:8)

Assure your teen that he can follow God's plan for his life by following certain steps:

1. Study the Bible so that the words of God are part of your daily life, easily recalled when you need to make decisions.

2. Ask for God's help.

3. Trust God in all things.

4. Evaluate choices in light of Scripture. Know the possible alternatives and consequences of a decision. Study the pros and cons.

5. Obey God when His will becomes clear.

Questions to Consider

1. Will my decision glorify God?

2. Am I qualified to follow through after a choice is made? Has God gifted me for this job?

3. Have I sought and considered the advice of qualified Christians?

4. Am I at peace with my decision and do I feel it will please God?

Further, remind your teen that when he accepts Jesus Christ as his Savior, the Holy Spirit lives inside him (John 7:37-39). Assure him that the Holy Spirit will guide and direct him to discover God's will as he seeks God's plan (John 14:26).

Other Bible resources: Ephesians 2:12-16; 1 Thessalonians 4:3; 5:18; 1 Peter 2:15; Psalm 40:8; Philippians 2:13; John 15:5.

32
I Am Scared Someone I Love Might Die. What Happens When People Die?

Andrew was alarmed by his mother's shocked tones as she talked on the telephone. Quickly, he walked into the kitchen. His mother slowly replaced the receiver, a stunned look on her face.

"What's wrong, Mom? What is it?" he asked.

His mother's eyes were clouded with pain as she looked up. "Andrew, it's my friend Laura. The receptionist called. Laura's dead—a car accident yesterday. She was driving home from an evening church meeting and the car flipped over and she was killed. A freak accident."

She looked down at her tensely clasped fingers. "I can hardly believe it. I see Laura every day and we just celebrated her birthday last week."

They sat side by side in silence.

Andrew moved closer and rested his hand on his mother's arm. "Mom," he said quietly. "I get scared sometimes that you and Dad might die suddenly like that. What happens when people die?"

Adult Response

You don't have to be frightened by death. When you believe in Jesus Christ, death is no longer a fearful thing. A Christian knows he is going to be with God in heaven forever. Paul tells us,

> Therefore we are always confident and know that as long as we are at home in the body we are away from the Lord. We live by faith, not by sight. We are confident, I say, and would prefer to be away from the body and at home with the Lord (2 Cor. 5:6-8).

So you are assured that when we who believe in Jesus die, we enter heaven with the Lord. There is only joy in that. Death is a natural part of life. It happens to each of us when the days God has planned for us to live on this earth are completed. Death is part of God's plan to bring us to Himself forever.

Jesus knew that death would be a source of worry for us. He teaches us to replace that worry with trust. In

Matthew 6:27 He asks His followers, "Who of you by worrying can add a single hour to his life?" And then comforts us, "Therefore do not worry about tomorrow, for tomorrow will worry about itself. Each day has enough trouble of its own" (v. 34).

It's true we all have to die someday, but remember that as long as we put our trust in Jesus, we will be reunited in heaven. When someone you love dies, God will be with you through your shock or confusion. You can trust His promise that He will help through the experience.

Additional Verses

1. "For I am convinced that neither death nor life, neither angels nor demons, neither the present nor the future, nor any powers, neither height nor depth, nor anything else in all creation, will be able to separate us from the love of God that is in Christ Jesus our Lord" (Rom. 8:38-39).

2. "When the perishable has been clothed with the imperishable, and the mortal with immortality, then the saying that is written will come true: " 'Death has been swallowed up in victory' " (1 Cor. 15:54).

3. "Precious in the sight of the Lord is the death of his saints" (Ps. 116:15).

Implications for the Older Child

Statistics show that in less than thirty years, 17.5 percent of Americans will be over age sixty-five. This information plus the fact that many married couples are waiting to have children means young people will likely see their loved ones age and also witness their death.

In the September 28, 1990, issue of *Family Circle* magazine, several studies reported that, in a list of teen concerns, the death of a parent was the top worry. Although teens are seeking independence, they want to have the assurance of parental support and love.

Be thankful that your child has expressed concern about death. Lead him to understand that death, like life, is in the Creator's plan and that it isn't to be feared. Christians who know the truth of Jesus Christ's death and resurrection no longer need fear death but can look forward to reunion with loved ones and the Lord Himself.

Assure your teen that in death there is hope. Although death came into the Garden of Eden, those who confess their sins and accept Jesus Christ as their personal Savior will live (2 Cor. 15:21-22). They will pass from life on earth to a heavenly celebration in the presence of the Lord Jesus Christ.

Further Scripture references: John 5:24; 8:51; Romans 6:23; 8:2; Revelation 1:18.

Section V
What Is God Like?
Questions About God

Section V
What Is God Like?
Questions About God

In the introduction to this book, I alluded to the impact our view of God has on all of life. If we grew up in a dysfunctional family, many of us had inadequate role models. Parental activities and mannerisms have given us a distorted view of God.

As parents we are uncomfortable with our imperfections. We shudder to think of the distortions concerning God that our children may be receiving as a result of our actions and attitudes. Yet we should accept this as a challenge to strive for a life more in accord with God's Word and greater dependence on the Holy Spirit's power to exemplify Christ's life through us.

At the same time, one of the most valuable gifts we can give our child is a correct view of God. Being imperfect, we can help our child identify the areas where we felt our actions or thoughts were not in accord with God's perfect character. When faced with a question or problem for which we have no answers, we can turn our child's attention to God who knows everything. At times, when we may be unloving or inattentive, we can admit our human inadequacies and tell our child of God whose love is changeless.

When worldly attitudes have infiltrated our thinking and we momentarily compromise by being unwilling to "take a stand" or "appear different" in work and social situations, we can tell them of our holy God. He is perfect in holiness and can help all of us by His Holy Spirit's power to take a stand in the face of peer pressure.

Lovingly direct your child to learn the character of our great God. Give him the privileged opportunity to develop an accurate picture of who He is—a picture that will prevent misconceptions that could cause him to stumble at a later time.

Examining God's character as revealed in His Word is the first step in knowing Him better. Help your child grow in his relationship with God by affording him opportunity to discover His person. You both will grow closer in the process.

33
Did God Really Create Everything?

Adult Response

Did you know that before God made the world, there was nothing? No earth, no skies, no animals, or people. God was all alone.

It was then God decided to create the world. "To create" means to make something from nothing and only God can do that. You and I cannot create anything because we are not God. If we decide to make something, we must start with something God has already created. If we bake a cake, we use water from rain, flour from wheat grain, and milk from cows. All of these were created by God.

Do you know how God created everything? Genesis 1:3,6 and 9 read, "And God said, 'Let there be light,' and there was light. And God said, 'Let there be an expanse between the waters to separate water from water.' And God said, 'Let the water under the sky be gathered to one place, and let dry ground appear.'"

Notice that each verse begins with "And God said . . . ." God said something and it happened. In the Book of Hebrews in chapter 11, verse 3 we read, "By faith we understand that the universe was formed at God's command, so that what is seen was not made out of what is visible." Only God can speak and see His words become real. That's because He is Creator.

Did you know that God: Father, Son, and Holy Spirit accomplished creation. We find in Genesis 1:26-27, "Then God said, 'Let *us* make man in *our* image, in *our* likeness"(author's italics). "Us" and "our" refer to more than one. God was referring to Himself as Father, Jesus Christ the Son, and Holy Spirit. So Jesus was involved in creation. The Bible tells us, "Through Him [Jesus Christ] all things were made; without him nothing was made that has been made" (John 1:3). We can know God our Heavenly Father better only if we learn about Jesus Christ His Son. We read in Colossians 1:15-17,

> He [Jesus] is the image of the invisible God, the first-born over all creation. For by him all things were created; things in heaven and on earth, visible and invisible, whether thrones or powers or rulers or authorities; all things were created by him and for him. He is before all things, and in him all things hold together.

God created everything and He holds it together every moment of every day.

Additional Verses

1. "I praise you because I am fearfully and wonderfully made; your works are wonderful, I know that full well" (Ps. 139:14).
2. "But in these last days he has spoken to us by his Son, whom he appointed heir of all things, and through whom he made the universe" (Heb. 1:2).
3. "But now, this is what the Lord says—he who created you, O Jacob, he who formed you, O Israel; 'Fear not for I have redeemed you; I have summoned you by name, you are mine' " (Isa. 43:1).

Further Insights

Josh McDowell writes in *Answers to Tough Questions,*

> The Scriptures do *not* teach there are three Gods; neither do they teach that God wears three different masks while acting out the drama of history. What the Bible does teach is stated in the doctrine of the Trinity as: there is *one* God who had revealed Himself in three persons, the

Father, the Son and the Holy Spirit, and these three persons are the one God,[1]

Myrna Alexander says,

> Consider the turbulent power of a hurricane, tornado or atomic explosion, the thundering crash of lightning or a magnificent waterfall.
>
> Now stretch your mind to imagine the fantastic power that restrains the sun from whirling into the earth, that holds the planets in orbit, the moon and stars in their paths. God, as Creator, is the source of all this power, equal to the combined power of all there is![2]

Implications for the Older Child

Since evolution is taught as a truth in most secular schools, your teen may have many questions and even doubts. Did we evolve from a lower form of life as some proclaim or did God create us in His own image? Dr. Louw Alberts, noted South African physics professor, in an interview in the March 1989 issue of *Decision* magazine said,

> Too often people, particularly young people, think that the atheistic view (of evolution) is the scientific one. There is nothing scientific about the viewpoint of an atheist. To say it all happened by chance cannot be proved or disproved.[3]

He went on to say that he believed "God brought this universe and man into being."[4] Many scientists agree with him. Knowledgeable Christians see no conflict between science and the Bible record. They are aware that change occurs within species through environmental, intellectual, and physical developments on the planet Earth, but they see these changes being used by God to reveal Himself and His universe to His children. They accept the biblical view of creation found in Genesis 1:1-31 where God created the heavens and earth and all things that dwell therein. He created humans in His own image. There is no conclusive scientific basis for human evolution across species barriers from a lower form of life on earth.

We know that the Bible is specific and the inspired Word of God. The Bible says in Genesis that God created everything. To try to explain how and when this was done is to try to explain the unexplainable. Remind your child there are some things we must accept by faith and that God has revealed Himself and His work through His inspiration to selected men who related it to the world through His Word, the Bible.

Other Scripture references: Mark 13:19-20; Romans 1:18-20; 2 Peter 3:3-8.

34
What Does It Mean that God Is Holy?

Adult Response

Holy means "set apart"—God is set apart from us because He is perfectly pure and spotless without a blemish. He is holy—different in every way. We see the holiness of God's character in Psalm 99, "Let them praise your great and awesome name—he is holy . . . Exalt the Lord our God and worship at his footstool; he is holy . . . Exalt the Lord our God and worship at his holy mountain for the Lord our God is holy" (vv. 3,5,9).

We read also that the Lord said to Moses, "Speak to the entire assembly of Israel and say to them: 'Be holy because I, the Lord your God, am holy'" (Lev. 19:2). God wants our companionship. That's the reason He had to remove our sin—it is unholy. It keeps us from God's presence.

This helps us understand that God sent His holy and perfect Son Jesus. He lived the perfect holy life we could not live and then died for our sins so we could know God.

As you grow to know God better each day, you will become more holy by the power of the Holy Spirit. Paul teaches, "You were taught, with regard to your former way of life, to put off your old self, which is being corrupted by its deceitful desires, to be made new in the attitude of your minds, and to put on the new self, created to be like God in true righteousness and holiness" (Eph. 4:22-24).

The Holy Spirit enables you to learn to live the holy life God plans for you, a life where you are set apart to do Christ's will.

Additional Verses

1. "Be imitators of God, therefore, as dearly loved children and live a life of love, just as Christ loved us and gave himself up for us as a fragrant offering and sacrifice to god" (Eph. 5:1-2).

2. "Now this is our boast: Our conscience testifies that we have conducted ourselves in the world, and especially in our relations with you, in the holiness and sincerity that are from God" (2 Cor. 1:12).

3. "You were taught, with regard to your former way of life, to put off your old self, which is being corrupted by its deceitful desires; to be made new in the attitudes of your minds, and to put on the new self, created to be like God in true righteousness and holiness" (Eph. 4:22-24).

Further Insights

Myrna Alexander says, "The central truth behind the purity and honor of all the attributes of God is that God is 'majestic in holiness' (Ex. 15:11). Therefore, the Scriptures refer to the holiness of God more than to any other attribute."[5]

Implications for the Older Child

Who can understand completely the holiness of God? The dictionary defines "holy" as characterized by perfection and transcendent; commanding absolute adoration and reverence. The Bible tells us that only God is holy (Rev. 15:4). Because God is sinless, we can trust His love, sovereignty, power, wisdom, faithfulness, and goodness. We can trust that when He forgives our sins, we are forgiven.

So your teen won't feel being holy is completely beyond comprehension, explain that although holiness is exclusive to God, a Christian should build a defense against sin by studying God's Word (Ps. 119:11) and depending on the Holy Spirit's power to help him reject sin's desires. Only God and the things of God are sinless, but as Christians we have the Holy Spirit's power to choose a life of righteousness and godliness.

By trying to be more like Jesus, we can reap the benefits of holiness. By knowing God and striving to live a righteous life in Christ, we will know peace (Job 22:21). We will receive strength to stand firm and act confidently (Dan. 11:32). By accepting the holiness of God, we will be free (John 8:32) and receive understanding (Prov. 9:10).

The goal of every Christian should be to reach toward holiness. John Bisagno writes, "True holiness will come when, as totally new creatures, we will be living in our glorified state in heaven with God."[6]

Other Scripture references: 1 Samuel 2:2; Leviticus 19:2; 11:44; Isaiah 6:3.

35
Is God Always "Just" in the Things He Does?

Adult Response

God's character never changes. Because of that He is always just. He always treats us fairly in every situation at all times and we can trust Him. In Deuteronomy 32:3-4, Moses declares, "I will proclaim the name of the Lord. Oh, praise the greatness of our God! He is the Rock, his works are perfect, and all his ways are just. A faithful God who does no wrong, upright and just is he."

God created Adam and Eve (as we learned in Gen. 1:26-27) without sin. When they obeyed Him and did only what God knew was good and best for them, everything was right and perfect.

God told them that there was only one thing that they could not do (Gen. 3:3). When Adam and Eve disobeyed God by doing the thing He had commanded them not to do, all of God's creation changed. Suddenly, man began to desire to do things that God didn't approve of. We call those ways "sin."

The reason Christ died for our sin was both because of God's justice and His mercy. Because He is just, God could not deny sin held a penalty that needed a payment. The payment was and is death.

Because God is merciful, He sent His son to pay the penalty so we would not have to die forever. Peter writes, "For Christ died for sins once for all, the righteous for the unrighteous, to bring you to God. He was put to death in the body but made alive by the Spirit" (1 Pet. 3:18).

God wanted to spend eternity (forever) with the people He created and loved. At the same time, the place where

God spends eternity is heaven. Nothing evil or bad can enter God's perfect heaven.

Now, what was God to do? Being just, He had to punish sin. Then, because He is a merciful God, He sent His Son Jesus Christ to earth to live the perfect life and then to die to pay the price for human sin.

Jesus was the only One with the power to do this and then to live again and join God in heaven for eternity. He made it possible for those who believe in Him to follow. God's mercy balances His justice.

Because He is completely just, God will always treat you fairly. When you don't understand something or feel unfairly treated by someone, remember that God sees the whole picture and will make certain that His fair and just purposes for your good will happen. At the same time, when you deserve God's justice for your sin, repent and call upon His mercy. Though you may experience sin's inevitable consequences, God will show you His mercy. "His mercy extends to those who fear him, from generation to generation" (Luke 1:50).

Additional Verses

1. "Good and upright is the Lord; therefore he instructs sinners in his ways. He guides the humble in what is right and teaches them his way. All the ways of the Lord are loving and faithful for those who keep the demands of his covenant" (Ps. 25:8-10).

2. "Yet the Lord longs to be gracious to you; he rises to show you compassion. For the Lord is a God of justice, Blessed are all who wait for him!" (Isa. 30:18).

3. "Righteousness and justice are the foundation of your throne; love and faithfulness go before you" (Ps. 89:14).

Further Insights

Paul E. Little says in *Know Why You Believe*,

> Jesus Christ was sinless. The caliber of his life was such that he was able to challenge his enemies with the question, 'Which of you convicts me of sin?' (John 8:46). He was met by silence, even though he addressed those who would have liked to point out a flaw in his character.[7]

Implications for the Older Child

One of the most difficult discussions you may have with a teen concerns sin and its consequences. In a permissive society like ours, the experience of sin is often downgraded or ignored. Yet we know that God is just, that He will judge sin. Justice is God's stand against sin which He hates. This is verified by the events in the Garden of Eden, the flood, and the destruction of Sodom and Gomorrah.

Humankind is sinful. In spite of this, God sacrificed His Son, Jesus Christ, on the cross to atone for our sinfulness. This is the supreme gesture of love. Yet we continue to sin and God continues to forgive.

God's justice is described in His gift of eternal life to sinners who have confessed their sin and asked for forgiveness. It is vital that your teen understand that if she meets God without accepting Christ, there is no hope. We cannot earn God's favor or salvation. There is no way we can do enough good things to compensate for our sins.

In the Bible, the justification of God is synonymous with His righteousness. Because of this we should all seek to be in right standing with God, by placing our faith in Jesus Christ. Explain that to be justified means to stand in a state of righteousness before God. Justification means that we recognize that Jesus is the Son of God and that He "was delivered for our offenses and raised again for our justification" (Rom. 4:25, KJV). By faith we are saved and by faith we are justified (Eph. 2:8-9) because God loves us and is just and righteous. Paul says, ". . . be reconciled to God. He made Him who knew no sin to be sin on our behalf, that we might become the righteousness of God in Him" (Eph. 5:20-21, NASB). In God's eyes, through Christ, we are accepted (Eph. 1:6). Our sins are forgiven.

Tell your teen that all she need do is believe in Jesus and God will honor that. There are consequences of sin but by God's grace we are saved (Eph. 2:5-8). Assure her that with the gift of forgiveness, guilt is dissolved and God acts mercifully toward us.

Other Scripture verses: John 5:30; Psalm 89:13; Proverbs 28:5; Romans 3:23; 8:1-2.

36
Is God Powerful Enough to Help Me?

Adult Response

King David wrote and sang many songs praising God. In Psalm 68:34 we find one that shows that he trusted God's power. "Proclaim the power of God, whose majesty is over Israel, whose power is in the skies."

Power is a strong word. Today, television and movie "superheroes" are portrayed as having great power, but we know that they aren't even real. Their power is imaginary. God's power is very real.

We know that Someone with great power created our universe and keeps the planets from colliding into one another. Weather changes are caused by Someone with power. This Someone is God.

In 1 Chronicles 29:11 we read,

Yours, O Lord, is the greatness and the power and the glory and the majesty and the splendor, for everything in heaven and earth is yours. Yours, O Lord, is the kingdom; you are exalted as head over all.

God uses His power to accomplish His good will in our lives. God can do anything. Nothing in our life is too hard for God to work out. Jeremiah gives us the words of God, "I am the Lord, the God of all mankind. Is anything too hard for me?" (32:27). Of course, nothing is too hard for the Creator.

When we believe in Jesus Christ, His Holy Spirit gives us power to do God's will. In Isaiah we read, "He gives strength to the weary and increases the power of the weak" (Isa. 40:29). During a time of great turmoil and stress, Paul wrote to the Philippians, "I can do everything through him who gives me strength" (Phil. 4:13).

If you ever find yourself in a situation that seems to be too big for anyone, even God, to handle, remember that all power belongs to God and He can and will do anything necessary to see that His powerful good will for you results.

Additional Verses

1. "Proclaim the power of God, whose majesty is over Israel, whose power is in the skies" (Ps. 68:34).

2. "All the people were amazed and said to each other, 'What is this teaching? With authority and power he gives orders to evil spirits and they come out'" (Luke 4:36).

3. "How God anointed Jesus of Nazareth with the Holy Spirit and power, and how he went around doing good and healing all who were under the power of the devil, because God was with him" (Acts 10:38).

4. "Ah, Sovereign Lord, you have made the heavens and the earth by your great power and outstretched arm. *Nothing* is too hard for you" (Jer. 32:17).

Further Insights

Pat Hershey Owen says,

> Remember: The promises are there. God both gives them and keeps them. But failure to realize and act on this principle, Jesus said, "is caused by your ignorance of the Scriptures and of God's power!" (Matt. 22:29, TLB). The error is multiplied if we, because of ignorance, do not know and teach the daily, personal, miraculous power of God.[8]

Myrna Alexander writes,

> Since all power belongs to God (Ps. 62:11), there is no such thing as one act being more difficult than another for God. Each of His acts is accomplished through the same effortless power. You see, it is just as easy for God to speak a universe into being as it is for Him to provide you with a needed new coat. There are no bounds to God's effortless power.[9]

Implications for the Older Child

Knowing God reigns supreme and is in control of all things and that He can never make a mistake should give us a sense of security and peace. The all-powerful God works in and through daily decisions for our good and His glory. "Consider what God has done: Who can straighten what he has made crooked? When times are good, be happy; but when times are bad consider: God has made the one as well as the other" (Eccl. 7:13-14).

God's power is also shown in Paul's letter to the Romans, "And we know that in all things God works for the good of those who love him, who have been called according to his purpose" (Rom. 8:28). What a blessed relief to know that we are never out of God's hands or His power even when we make poor choices! A poor choice can be used by God to help us understand His saving power.

To a teen interested in science, relate God's power to

that of nature, shown in the turbulent and destructive force found in hurricanes, lightning, and floods. Mention the energy of solar power that turns the earth green in summer and brown in fall. Remind him the Creator is the source of all this power and more. We have not been able to find the limits of God's power.

One of God's powerful acts is shown through the new Christian whom He changes into a new and different person when he accepts Jesus Christ as his Savior. Jesus possesses the power of God (Matt. 28:18), and His Spirit displays Christ's power in our life. As Paul reminded the Romans, "You, however, are controlled not by the sinful nature but by the Spirit, if the Spirit of God lives in you" (Rom. 8:9).

Other Scripture references: Genesis 1; Psalm 33:6-11; 100:3; Colossians 1:16-17.

37
Is God Really Good?

Adult Response

David encourages us to "Give thanks to the Lord, for he is good his love endures forever" (Ps. 118:1). Everything God does is good. Being good, He plans good things for our lives. In James 1:17 we learn, "Every good and perfect gift is from above, coming down from the Father of the heavenly lights, who does not change like shifting shadows."

God promises that the plans He has for us are for our good and that He will work out even the bad things that happen to us so that they will result in good. "And we know that in all things God works for the good of those who love him, who have been called according to his purpose" (Rom. 8:28).

Jesus reminds us, "I am the good shepherd; I know my sheep and my sheep know me—just as the Father knows me and I know the Father—and I lay down my life for the sheep" (John 10:14-15). You can remember that you have a shepherd, Jesus Christ, who will care for you just as a shepherd in the fields cares for his sheep. His care is good.

When troubles come and bad things happen to you in life, always remember that God is good, that He gives good gifts. He will work with you to solve the problem in order to accomplish His good purpose in your life. The world we live in is sinful and the enemy, Satan, attempts to cause trouble in our lives. Never forget Jesus said, "I have told you these things, so that in me you may have peace. In this world you will have trouble. But take heart! I have overcome the world" (John 16:33).

Additional Verses

1. "Taste and see that the Lord is good; blessed is the man who takes refuge in him" (Ps. 34:8).

2. "You intended to harm me, but God intended it for good to accomplish what is now being done" (Gen. 50:20).

3. "Good and upright is the Lord; therefore he instructs sinners in his ways. He guides the humble in what is right and teaches them his way (Ps. 25:8-9).

Further Insights

Joyce Milburn, in *Helping Your Children Love Each Other*, says,

> God is the perfect parent. He is loving, protective, and sensitive to our every need, yet firm, honest and fair. Our Heavenly Father's care for us embodies the prime example of everything an earthly parent could ever hope to be.[10]

Grace M. Hunt writes,

No one is wise enough to answer all family needs in himself. The distinguishing mark of a Christian family is that they know Who does have the answers. . . . It is important to God because through it the children He gives us are molded in godliness. It is a witness to the world of God's (goodness) and grace.[11]

Implications for the Older Child

The dictionary defines "goodness" as excellence of character, generous and kindly feelings, benevolence. We can be comforted to know that God is absolutely good, that He has never done anything that is not good. We can depend on His goodness for our lives. "The Lord is good, a refuge in times of trouble, He cares for those who trust in Him" (Nah. 1:7).

Encourage your teen to think of God's goodness and to depend on it every day. No matter what happens in life, God's goodness will persevere. Through God's grace, we receive His love and goodness.

Myrna Alexander writes, "Because He [God] possesses unlimited power and is perfectly in control of all things, God may always accomplish His totally wise and good plans for you."[12] In the Bible we read, "The Lord is good to all; he has compassion on all he has made" (Ps. 145:8).

When searching for the goodness of God, we need only look at His sacrifice of His Son, Jesus Christ, to atone for our sins. Remind your son or daughter that because God is good and merciful, we should reflect that goodness in our own relationships.

Other Scripture references: John 3:16; Romans 8:28,32; Ephesians 1:5-8.

38
Does God Know Everything?

You can be comforted by learning that God does know everything. He knows all about you. He knows what you think before you say it. He knows how you feel. He knows what you need. He knew you and loved you before you were ever born. He knows and loves you every day.

David says in Psalm 139:2,4: "You know when I sit and when I rise; you perceive [understand] my thoughts from afar. Before a word is on my tongue, you know it completely, O Lord."

You can have peace in knowing that nothing escapes God's notice. Because He wishes only good for you, you need never fear His presence. We learn in Psalm 147:5, "Great is our Lord and mighty in power; his understanding has no limit."

Jesus tells us, ". . . for your Father knows what you need before you ask him" (Matt. 6:8). The writer of Hebrews also tells us, "Nothing in all creation is hidden from God's sight. Everything is uncovered and laid bare before the eyes of the him to whom we must give account" (Heb. 4:13).

Whatever happens to you, you can be sure that God knows and understands both the situation and your feelings. "Cast your anxiety on him for He cares for you," Peter tells us (1 Pet. 5:7). Next time you wonder if anyone knows or understands, remember that God does. He's with you always and not only knows of your concerns but has the power to do something about them.

Additional Verses

1. "For the Lord watches over the way of the righteous but the way of the wicked will perish" (Ps.1:6).

2. "If you, then, though you are evil, know how to give good gifts to your children, how much more will your Father in heaven give good gifts to those who ask him!" (Matt. 7:11).

3. "I am the good shepherd. I know my sheep and my sheep know me—just as the Father knows me and I know the Father—and I lay down my life for the sheep" (John 10:14).

Implications for the Older Child

A teen prays, thinking, _How can God hear my prayers and all the other prayers being made at this exact moment_? This thought may have crossed your mind also. We who are amazed at modern computers because of their stored information cannot comprehend the more complex mind of God.

The answer is in God's Word. The psalmist cried, "O Lord, you have searched me and you know me. You know when I sit and when I rise; you perceive my thoughts from afar. You discern my going out and my lying down; you are familiar with all my ways" (Ps. 139:1-3).

God's omniscience is revealed in the fact that He knows everything that has or will happen since the beginning of time: past, present and future. Because this is incomprehensible for the human mind, it must be accepted by faith.

With faith, you can assure your child that God loves him and desires only the best for him in spite of his faults and mistakes, all of which are known to God. "Nothing in all creation is hidden from God's sight. Everything is uncovered and laid bare before the eyes of him to whom we must give account" (Heb. 4:13).

The fact that God knows us better than we know ourselves means He can help us when we don't know how to help ourselves. He knows our deepest needs and can meet them, needs that we may not even be aware of. There is comfort in His knowledge of us.

Remind your teen that the Holy Spirit is with us at all times, interceding for us, helping us. So God knows our problems and troubles and encourages us as He works out His plan for our lives. "For those God foreknew he also predestined to be conformed to the likeness of his Son" (Rom. 8:29).

Other Scripture verses: Job 23:10; Ezekiel 11:5; Acts 15:18; Hebrews 4:13; Jeremiah 11:20.

39
Is God Everywhere?

Because God is Spirit, He is able to be everywhere at all times. Someone once called God the Invisible Reality. Although we cannot see Him, He is with us. Understanding this, David wrote, "Where can I go from your Spirit? Where can I flee from your presence? If I go up to the heavens, you are there; if I make my bed in the depths, you are there" (Ps. 139:7-8).

Jesus reminded His disciples of this fact before He ascended to sit at the right hand of our Father God.

> Therefore go and make disciples of all nation, baptizing them in the name of the Father and of the Son and of the Holy Spirit, and teaching them to obey everything I have commanded you. And surely I am with you always, to the very end of the age (Matt. 28:19-20).

Whether you are lonely or afraid, joyful or anxious,

God is there to share your pain, sorrow, joy, or anticipation. He is there to guide, comfort and join you in every experience of life. You can believe in him and trust Him in everything.

Additional Verses

1. "If I rise on the wings of the dawn, if I settle on the far side of the sea, even there your hand will guide me" (Ps. 139:9-10).

2. "But now, this is what the Lord says—he who created you, O Jacob, he who formed you, O Israel. '... When you pass through the waters, I will be with you' " (Isa. 43:1-2).

3. "Humble yourselves before the Lord, and he will lift you up" (Jas. 4:10).

4. "God is our refuge and our strength, an ever-present help in trouble" (Ps. 46:1).

Implications for the Older Child

The teen years are a time for questions and doubts. Teens may wonder, *Where is God, anyway?* Explaining the omnipresence of God may be difficult since, being literal, they may accept the erroneous concept that if you can't see, touch, or hear something, it doesn't exist. How can God whom we can't see be with us at all times? What does it mean that God is present in three forms: Father, Son, and Holy Spirit?

Explain that through faith, we accept the Trinity of God, our Guide, Protector, Father, Friend. Jesus, speaking to Philip said, "Don't you believe that I am in the Father and that the Father is in me? The words I say to you are not just my own. Rather it is the Father, living in me, who is doing his work" (John 14:10).

Unlike humans, God, able to transcend time, space, and form, is the same yesterday, today, and tomorrow, forever. His Holy Spirit (Christ's Spirit) lives in the heart of Christians, ever ready to guide and help in times of trouble or indecision.

What joy to know that God is everywhere. "O Lord, you have searched me and you know me. You know when I sit and when I rise; you perceive my thoughts from afar." Where can I go from your Spirit? Where can I flee from your presence? If I go up to the heavens, you are there; if I make my bed in the depths, you are there" (Ps. 139:1-2,7-8).

Encourage your teen to think of herself as being surrounded by God who lives in her heart and is everywhere else she may go. Rejoice in this fact as the Psalmist did, "You have made known to me the path of life; you will fill me with joy in your presence, with eternal pleasures at your right hand" (Ps. 16:11).

Finally, remind her of Jesus' words, "And surely I am with you always, to the very end of the age" (Matt. 28:20).

Other Scripture verses: Hebrews 13:5; 1 Kings 8:27; Acts 17:28; Romans 8:35,38-39.

40
Is God Faithful? Can I Depend on Him?

Faithfulness is one of God's character qualities. He will never let you down or disappoint you. God can be trusted completely and depended on totally. The prophet Jeremiah wrote, "Because of the Lord's great love we are not consumed, for his compassions never fail. They are new every morning; great is your faithfulness" (Lam. 3:22-23).

Moses tells us of God's faithfulness, "Know therefore that the Lord your God is God; he is the faithful God, keeping his covenant of love to a thousand generations of those who love him and keep his commands" (Deut. 7:9). Because we are His precious children, He will faithfully love us at all times. Paul wrote to the Corinthians, "God, who has called you into fellowship with his Son Jesus Christ our Lord, is faithful" (1 Cor. 1:9).

It is a comfort to know that God will always care for you throughout your life at all times. He will help you overcome temptation and live the life He desires for you. You can trust Him to do these things because He is faithful. You can also trust His promises found in His Word because His character never changes, and He is faithful in everything. "All your commands are trustworthy," the psalmist declares (Ps. 119:86).

Additional Verses

1. "He remembers his covenant forever, the word he commanded, for a thousand generations" (Ps. 105:8).

2. "Let us hold unswervingly to the hope we profess, for he who promised is faithful"(Heb. 10:23).

3. "If we are faithless, he will remain faithful, for he cannot disown himself" (2 Tim. 2:13).

4. "Your word, O Lord, is eternal: it stands firm in the heavens. Your faithfulness continues through all generations" (Ps. 119:89-90).

Implications for the Older Child

A teen may ask, "How do I know I can depend on God?" He may relate the times he felt his prayers went unanswered. How do you assure your child that God is faithful and that He keeps His promises at all times, that Jesus' words, "Ask and it will be given to you" (Matt. 7:7), can be trusted?

You can assure your teenager with God's Word, "Because of the Lord's great love we are not consumed, for his compassions never fail. They are new every morning; great is your faithfulness" (Lam. 3:22-23), or "God is our refuge and strength, an ever present help in trouble" (Ps. 46:1), "Be my rock of refuge, to which I can always go; give the command to save me for you are my rock and my fortress" (Ps. 71:3).

When we ask, God answers with the solution that is best for us. Even when it's not the answer we wish, He gives us the strength to take the bad moment and change it to something better. For each prayer there is an answer because God is faithful. At times, He simply removes the source of the problem.

For example, a young teen was causing his Christian parents much concern and unhappiness. The child wasn't abusing drugs or running with the wrong crowd. Instead, he was insolent, obstinate, and argumentative. No matter what his dad said or asked, he rebelled.

The parents prayed for God's guidance. Trusting His faithfulness, they waited, trying to be tolerant and understanding of their son's negative behavior.

Then one day near the end of the school year, the boy was offered an opportunity to attend a month-long sports camp. By the time he returned home, his parents had had time to think about the relationship while the teen, homesick and lonely, realized that his parents were important to him. The separation didn't solve all the problems, but it helped both parents and teen look at the behavior from a different perspective.

Help your child experience the good news that our faithful God works every day in our lives. Remind him of the good things that God has done for him and others and that when bad times come into our lives it's often because we have made poor decisions. God is always faithful in letting us make decisions good and bad, but He never leaves us to suffer alone.

Encourage your teen to place his faith in God, to acknowledge His faithfulness and then trust Him to work for his good throughout life.

Other Scripture verses: 1 Thessalonians 5:24; Deuteronomy 7:9; Revelation 19:11; Psalm 36:7.

Notes

Section I

1. Ross Campbell, *How to Really Love Your Child* (Victor Books, 1977), 31.

2. Walter Wagner, *Heavenly Humor for All God's Children*, 54.

3. Anne Gillilard, *Understanding Preschoolers* (Old Tappan, N.J.: Revell, 1984).

4. Richard Strauss, *Confident Children and How They Grow* (Wheaton, Ill.: Tyndale House, 1975), 33.

5. Ray and Anne Ortland, "Three Things Children Need from Parents," *Parents & Children* (Victor Books, 1986), 87.

6. Paul Heiderbrecht, "Building Self-Esteem in Your Child," *Parents & Children* (Victor Books, 1986), 537.

7. Betty N. Chase, *Discipline Them, Love Them* (Elgin, Ill.: David C. Cook, 1982), 81.

8. Pat Hershey Owen, *The Idea Book for Mothers* (Wheaton, Ill.: Tyndale House, 1981), 113.

9. Campbell, 55.

10. Herbert Scott, "Coping with Loneliness Through Prayer," *Missionary Crusader*, Sept. 1985, 12.

11. Gladys M. Hunt, *Focus on Family Life* (Grand Rapids: Baker Book House, 1970), 37.

12. Eileen Guder, *Deliver Us From Fear* (Waco, Tex.: Word Books, 1976), 9-24, 47-62.

13. Elizabeth Skoglund, *Can I Talk To You?* (Gospel Light Publications, 1977), 110.

14. Tony Campolo, "How Peer Pressure Works," *Parents & Children* (Victor Books, 1986), 529.

15. James Dobson, *Hide or Seek*, Rev. Ed. (Old Tappan, N.J.: Fleming H. Revell, 1979), 59.

16. Ibid., 80.

17. Ibid., 84.

18. Wayne Rice, "Every Kid Needs an Adult Friend," *Parents & Children* (Victor Books, 1986), 387.

19. Judith Shelly, "Spiritual Needs of Sick Children," *Parents & Children* (Victor Books, 1986), 685.

20. Elizabeth Catherine Baker-Smith, "The Impact of Illness on the

Family and the Ministry of the Christian Community," *Encyclopedia of Christian Parenting* (Old Tappan, N.J.: Revell, 1984).

21. Norm Wakefield, *A Happier Family* (Gospel Light Publications, 1977), 124.

22. Campbell, 131.

23. Ibid.

24. Ibid.

25. John Albright, "Mom, What's Wrong with Me?" *Parents & Children* (Victor Books, 1986), 552.

26. Ibid, 554.

27. Dobson, 90.

28. Judson Swihart, "The Importance of Grandparents," *Parents & Children* (Victor Books, 1986), 495.

Section II

1. Miriam Huffman Rockness, *Keep These Things—Ponder Them In Your Heart* (New York: Doubleday, 1979).

2. Richard Strauss, *Confident Children and How They Grow* (Wheaton, Ill.: Tyndale House, 1975).

3. Roger Allen and Ron Rose, *Common Sense Discipline* (Fort Worth: Worthy Publishing, 1986), 119.

4. Ross Campbell, *Kids Who Follow, Kids Who Don't* (Victor Books, 1987), 64.

5. James Dobson, *The Strong-willed Child*, (Wheaton, Ill.: Tyndale House, 1978), 204.

6. Gladys M. Hunt, *Focus on Family Life* (Grand Rapids: Baker Book House, 1970), 51.

7. Tim LaHaye, *The Battle for the Family* (Old Tappan, N.J.: Fleming H. Revell, 1982), 162.

8. Allen and Rose, 120.

9. Dean and Grace Merrill, *Together At Home* (Nashville: Thomas Nelson Publishers, 1985), 169-70.

10. Ted Ward, *Values Begin at Home* (Victor Books, 1989), 51.

11. Stuart Alan Capons, *Parents Guide to Teenagers.*

12. Paul Lewis, *40 Ways to Teach Your Child Values* (Wheaton, Ill.: Tyndale House, 1985), 127.

13. Allen and Rose, 154.

14. Gary Hunt, *Surviving the Teenage Years* (San Bernadino, Calif.: Here's Life Publications, 1985)

15 Ibid.

16. Paul Ekman, *Why Children Lie* (New York: Macmillan, 1989).

17. Gladys M. Hunt, *Focus on Family Life*, (Grand Rapids: Baker Book House, 1970), 16.

18. Allen and Rose, 28.

19. Ward, 128.

20. Billy Graham, *My Answer*, syndicated newspaper column, April, 1991.

21. Gordon W. Allport, "Psychology of Personality," from Hall, Calvins, Goodman, and Lindsey, *Theories of Personality,* 456.

Section III

1. Ted Ward, *Values Begin at Home* (Victor Books, 1989), 100.

2. Roger Allen and Ron Rose, *Common Sense Discipline* (Fort Worth: Worthy Publishing, 1986), 123.

3. Kevin Huggins, *Parenting Adolescents* (NavPress, 1989), 56.

4. Arthur Murray, *How to Raise Your Child for Christ* (Bethany Fellowship, 1975), 222.

5. Dick Day, *Discipling the Young Person* (San Bernardino, Calif.: Here's Life Publishers, 1985), 75.

6. Judith Allen Shelly, *The Spiritual Needs of Children* (Downers Grove, Ill.: Inter-Varsity Press), 19.

7. "America's Youth: Mission Field of the '90's"

8. Ron and Judy Blue, *Money Matters for Parents and Their Kids* (Atlanta: Oliver Nelson, 1988), 45-46.

Section IV

1. Paul Lewis, *40 Ways to Teach Your Children Values,* (Living Books, Tyndale, 1985), 177.

2. Paul E. Little, *Know Why You Believe* (Downers Grove, Ill.: Inter-Varsity, 1968), 57-58.

3. Judith Allen Shelly, *The Spiritual Needs of Children*, (Downer's Grove, Ill.: Intervarsity Press, 1982), 19.

4. Lewis, 180.

5. Ted Ward, *Values Begin at Home*, (Victor Books, 1989), 88-89.

6. E. V. Hill, "The Power of Prayer in Youth Ministry."

7. Michael W. Smith, *Old Enough to Know* (Dallas, Tex.: Word Pub., 1987), 133.

8. Raymond and Dorothy Moore, *Home-grown Kids* (Waco, Tex.: Word Books, 1981).

9. Billy Graham, *My Answer,* syndicated newspaper column, April 11, 1991.

Section V

1. Josh McDowell and Don Stewart, *Answers to Tough Questions* (San Bernardino, Calif.: Here's Life Publishers, 1980), 71.

2. Myrna Alexander, *Behold Your God* (Grand Rapids: Zondervan Publishers, 1978), 36.

3. Lou Alberts, *Decision*, March 1989.

4. Ibid.

5. Alexander, 67.

6. John Bisagno, *God Is* (Victor Books, 1983), 45.

7. Paul E. Little, *Know Why You Believe* (Downer's Grove. Ill.: Inter-Varsity Press, 1968), 19.

8. Pat Hershey Owen, *The Idea Book for Mothers* (Wheaton, Ill.: Tyndale House, 1981), 164.

9. Alexander, 37.

10. Joyce Milburn, *Helping Your Children Love Each Other* (Bethany House, 1983), 23.

11. Grace M. Hunt, *Focus on Family Life* (Grand Rapids: Baker Book House, 1970), 13.

12. Alexander, 46.